"This book arrives at a critical moment when educational leaders are grappling with how to authentically center educational equity while bridging divides, expanding belonging, and supporting the social and emotional well-being of their communities. Cassetta uses case studies to brilliantly illustrate how social awareness requires us to lean into curiosity, consistently check our assumptions and engage with the historical, cultural, and systemic forces that shape every interaction in our schools. In the case examples and throughout the book, you will see how leading transformation requires simultaneous attention to both the technical and the deeply relational dimensions of change that impact peoples' ability and willingness to engage skillfully and effectively.

As a long-time leadership coach and trauma therapist, I deeply appreciate how the acknowledgement that the state of our own nervous systems, our presence, language, and decisions literally shape the extent to which people feel safe around us. This awareness is critical as a felt sense of safety is a precondition to healthy social engagement, collaboration, and learning. Leading with social and nervous system awareness is especially important for leaders working with students and staff who carry the daily metabolic cost of navigating marginalization within our current systems.

For any leader committed to leading meaningful transformation, this book provides both a framework and relatable examples to guide leaders to do the deep inside out work that lasting change requires."

Kathleen Osta, LCSW, SEP, Managing Director,<br>National Equity Project

"Equity requires a redesigned kind of relationship—one where power, trust, and knowledge flow freely and without friction. I truly believe that the schoolhouse—especially the public school—holds immense promise for adults to model equity, shared ownership, and power with the children in our classrooms. The Social and Emotional Core of Equity Leadership offers a powerful roadmap for any educator or school leader seeking to deepen their skills in designing and developing equitable relationships."

Caroline Hill, 228Accelerator

"I became an educator to fight for social justice, yet I've found through the years that the way we do the work often reinforces the status quo. Finding my way through that as a K-8 teacher and then a middle school principal has always been one of the hardest parts of the work. There is very little practical guidance for how to make the means match the ends. This book is full of concrete tools and strategies grounded in Emotional Intelligence, SEL and DEI theory and practice. Cassetta combines her deep experience as an educator with her excellent prose to give us something new in the sector to guide school leader practice and development."

Matt Taylor, Founder and CEO, Noble Story Group

"Gianna Cassetta's The Social and Emotional Core of Equity Leadership is a powerfully humanistic and timely call to action for school leaders to do the deep inner work that is imperative for sustainable, equity-centered change. By integrating social and emotional learning, the analysis of issues of power, and root causes of inequity, Cassetta transcends comfortable solutions by offering a roadmap to generate meaningful community where all members belong and student voices are lifted up. This book invites us to be deeply reflective, stretch beyond what has seemed comfortable, disrupt inequity, and lead authentically, grounded in empathy, humility, and courage. It's essential reading for every educator committed to justice."

Kristina A. Hesbol, PhD, Associate Professor,
Educational Leadership and Policy Studies, University of
Denver, Founding Director, Center for Innovative
Rural Collaborative Leadership Education (CIRCLE)

"The Social and Emotional Core of Equity Leadership is a wake-up call for every leader. Cassetta pulls no punches as she dares us to do the real work: inner reckoning and outer repair to dismantle the systems we've been complicit in. It's a blueprint for leading with both heart and spine. Read it if you're done playing it safe."

Annie Azarloza, Education Leader, M.Ed

# The Social and Emotional Core of Equity Leadership

*The Social and Emotional Core of Equity Leadership: A Guide for Driving Change in Schools* is a practical guide for educational leaders committed to creating inclusive schools where all students feel a sense of belonging. Challenging traditional approaches to social and emotional learning (SEL), this book argues that adult SEL must be rooted in equity and justice, not compliance or neutrality.

Through vivid case studies, research-informed frameworks, and a structured reflection tool, readers explore how inner work (like identity reflection, emotional self-awareness, and bias interruption) must fuel outer work (like policy change, community engagement, and institutional redress). Organized around five core SEL domains, the book offers concrete strategies for making equity actionable, particularly in moments of resistance, controversy, or discomfort.

Written for principals, district leaders, and school leadership teams, this book is ideal for those navigating real-world pressures while striving to lead with clarity and conscience. Whether you're rethinking discipline systems, addressing bias in dress codes, or responding to exclusion that flies under the radar, this book helps you lead more skillfully and justly.

**Gianna Cassetta** has been a classroom teacher, a school founder and leader, and a district-level leader. She is a certified Goleman EI Emotional Intelligence Coach and an International Coaching Federation Associate Certified Coach. She founded The Plain Red Horse Coaching and Consulting, where she supports parallel and equity-focused pathways to social and emotional development for children and adults.

# Equity and Social Justice in Education Series
## Paul C. Gorski, Series Editor

Routledge's Equity and Social Justice in Education series is a publishing home for books that apply critical and transformative equity and social justice theories to the work of on-the-ground educators. Books in the series describe meaningful solutions to the racism, white supremacy, economic injustice, sexism, heterosexism, transphobia, ableism, neoliberalism, and other oppressive conditions that pervade schools and school districts.

**Anti-Oppressive Universal Design for Teachers**
Building Equitable Classrooms
*Diana Ma*

**Integrating Educator Well-Being, Growth, and Evaluation**
Four Foundations for Leaders
*Lori Cohen and Elizabeth Denevi*

**Humanizing Pedagogies with Multilingual Learners**
Transforming Teaching in the Content Areas
*Kara Mitchell Viesca and Nancy L. Commins*

**From Empathy to Action**
Empowering K-6 Students to Create Change Through Reading, Writing, and Research
*Chris Hass, Katie Kelly, and Lester Laminack*

**Promoting Equitable Math Instruction**
Exploring Elementary Teachers' Stories
*Monica L. Gonzalez and Alesia Mickle Moldavan*

**The Social and Emotional Core of Equity Leadership**
A Guide for Driving Change in Schools
*Gianna Cassetta*

# The Social and Emotional Core of Equity Leadership

## A Guide for Driving Change in Schools

Gianna Cassetta

Routledge
Taylor & Francis Group
NEW YORK AND LONDON

Designed cover image: Getty Images

First published 2026
by Routledge
605 Third Avenue, New York, NY 10158

and by Routledge
4 Park Square, Milton Park, Abingdon, Oxon, OX14 4RN

*Routledge is an imprint of the Taylor & Francis Group, an informa business*

© 2026 Gianna Cassetta

The right of Gianna Cassetta to be identified as author of this work has been asserted in accordance with sections 77 and 78 of the Copyright, Designs and Patents Act 1988.

All rights reserved. No part of this book may be reprinted or reproduced or utilised in any form or by any electronic, mechanical, or other means, now known or hereafter invented, including photocopying and recording, or in any information storage or retrieval system, without permission in writing from the publishers.

*Trademark notice*: Product or corporate names may be trademarks or registered trademarks, and are used only for identification and explanation without intent to infringe.

ISBN: 978-1-032-82334-8 (pbk)
ISBN: 978-1-003-51035-2 (ebk)

DOI: 10.4324/9781003510352

Typeset in Palatino
by Newgen Publishing UK

# Contents

*Acknowledgments* . . . . . . . . . . . . . . . . . . . . . . . . . . . . . *xi*
*Meet the Author* . . . . . . . . . . . . . . . . . . . . . . . . . . . . . . . *xii*

Introduction . . . . . . . . . . . . . . . . . . . . . . . . . . . . . . . . . 1

**Part 1**
**Foundations of SEL** . . . . . . . . . . . . . . . . . . . . . . . . . . . . 15

1  A Tiered Approach Starts with All Students in Mind . . . . . . . . . . . . . . . . . . . . . . . . . . . . . . . . . . . . . 17

2  Creating the Conditions That Support SEL . . . . . . . . . . . 36

**Part 2**
**The Inner Work of SEL We Need to do The Outer Work of Equity and Justice** . . . . . . . . . . . . . . . . . . . . . . . 53

3  Self-Awareness . . . . . . . . . . . . . . . . . . . . . . . . . . . . . . . 55

4  Self-Management . . . . . . . . . . . . . . . . . . . . . . . . . . . . . 88

5  Social Awareness . . . . . . . . . . . . . . . . . . . . . . . . . . . . 117

6  Relationship Management . . . . . . . . . . . . . . . . . . . . . 138

7  Responsible Decision-Making . . . . . . . . . . . . . . . . . . 160

**8 Putting It Into Practice: A Reflection Tool for
Equity-Centered Leadership** ........................176

*Conclusion: Belonging Without Exception*     *186*
*Bibliography*     *190*

# Acknowledgments

This book would not exist without the insight and support of people whose names may not appear on the cover but whose fingerprints are on the pages.

Thank you to the educators who allowed me to coach them, share their stories, ask hard questions, challenge assumptions, and make time for reflection in the middle of impossible days. Your leadership shaped these pages.

To the brilliant women who've been a part of my professional (and sometimes personal) life and to the researchers and facilitators whose work has shaped me from a distance, your influence shows up in how I think, what I question, and where I choose to act.

Thank you to Margaret Wilson for reading very drafty chapters early on, and Angela Stepancic for reading a chapter I was nervous about much later on.

To my colleagues at Noble Story Group and Beyond EI—from whom I continue to learn and evolve my thinking about coaching, emotional intelligence, and adult SEL—thank you for being thoughtful and rigorous in your practice. You've helped me imagine what this work can look like when angled with a particular intention.

To my series editor, Paul Gorski, thank you for your steady guidance and unwavering commitment to equity. Your feedback pushed me to be sharper and braver.

To my husband, Marc Waxman, for consistently encouraging me to do not what is easiest or most practical, but what is most meaningful. Thank you for being a true partner in this work and in life.

Finally, to my readers, navigating the daily tension between what is and what should be: I hope you see yourself in some of the stories, find what's here useful and practical, and feel supported as you do the work that matters for your students and families, colleagues, and yourself.

# Meet the Author

Gianna began her teaching career in New York City, becoming one of the state's first twenty-five National Board Certified teachers. Her passion for education led her to co-found and lead one of only five public-to-charter conversion schools in NYC. She helped launch the Office of School Reform and Innovation at Denver Public Schools as Director of Leadership Development before starting a school in Denver.

She co-authored *Classroom Management Matters: The Social and Emotional Learning Approach That Children Deserve*, *No More Taking Away Recess and Other Problematic Discipline Practices*, and *The Caring Teacher: Strategies for Working Through Your Own Difficulties with Students*.

Gianna founded and leads The Plain Red Horse Coaching and Consulting, LLC, where she supports parallel and equity-focused pathways to social and emotional development for children and adults. She partners with leaders to apply these principles in their practice, driving institutional change and building communities rooted in belonging and justice. Gianna is a certified Beyond EI (formerly Goleman EI) Emotional Intelligence Coach and an International Coaching Federation Associate Certified Coach. She lives on a small hobby farm in New England with her human family and her ever-growing non-human family of adopted equines, canines, felines, and fowl.

# Introduction

If you asked most school leaders, in our best moments, what kind of community we envision for students, we'd likely describe a place where they're engaged, learning, and thriving. A place where they're known. A place of belonging. We might use different words, but I don't know a school leader who doesn't want that.

I wanted that. Over twenty-five years ago, when I first heard the term social and emotional learning (SEL), I was leading a K–8 school in New York City, working with my staff to reimagine the relationships between adults and students. Could we shift from a school where adults tightly managed behavior to one where students experienced greater independence and autonomy? Where students made decisions because they believed in them, not just because adults told them what was right? Where they felt the school belonged to them as much as to us? Where every student experienced belonging?

Like most educators, I cared deeply about my students. I loved teaching, designing policies I believed would help them, laughing with them, and playing with them. They deserved access to caring classrooms where they could grow academically, artistically, physically, socially, and emotionally.

We built long-term partnerships with SEL organizations to embed these practices throughout the school, in classrooms, hallways, the cafeteria, and the playground. In many ways, the results were lovely. Students seemed happy. They built friendships, felt close to teachers, and were confident in their learning and abilities. They set personal goals, managed projects, made thoughtful choices, and helped determine restitution when harm occurred. These were meaningful accomplishments.

And still, in most classrooms, one or two students weren't *compliant*, and I use that word intentionally. We tend to over-value and over-reward compliance. When students didn't follow routines, complete work, or respond to redirection, we adults assumed something was wrong with them. We had no structure or expectations for adult SEL. So when we got frustrated, we externalized it. We didn't ask what was happening within us, what emotion we were feeling, or what story we were telling ourselves. Instead, we focused on getting students to meet our expectations.

Shawn was one of those students. The district placed him at our school in the middle of sixth grade after multiple fights at his previous school. That kind of transfer was common, especially for Black and Brown students. They were moved if a student was suspended enough or if the principal complained loudly enough. On his first day, Shawn got into a fistfight in the science lab when another student stepped on his foot. The pattern continued. He fought, argued with teachers, and was regularly disruptive. By the end of seventh grade, his mother withdrew him and enrolled him elsewhere.

I remember feeling indignant that other principals could off-load students and expect us to absorb the impact. I was angry at the superintendent's indifference to our school culture and at Shawn for not just behaving.

I don't remember questioning the systems that made it so easy and normal for schools to discard kids. To say *you don't belong here*, and *you're not my problem*. I didn't think much about what it meant for Shawn to be sent away from a school that may never have welcomed him, only to arrive at another where no one considered how to welcome him either.

With a better understanding of what it takes to create true belonging, we could have done more. We could have seen Shawn's arrival as a developmental process, not a disruption. Someone could have greeted him at the door, given him a tour, or paired him with a buddy. We could have checked in with him regularly and asked about his interests, goals, and experiences.

We could have responded to his needs in ways that nurtured trust and growth.

As adults, we could have acknowledged our own feelings, frustrations, fears, and resentments without letting them define our approach. Many things can be true at once: the system can be unjust, leadership can be exhausting, and students can be challenging. But that doesn't mean we need to continue cycles of harm. We could have steadied ourselves, supported each other, and shown up for Shawn. We could have believed in his potential and committed to helping him realize it.

Over time, I've learned how to operationalize these commitments through equity-centered adult SEL. This book is about that. While anyone working in schools may find it helpful, it is written with school leaders in mind.

As leaders, we must understand that centering equity is inseparable from practicing adult SEL. This work requires more than surface-level commitments. It asks us to interrogate how things have always been done and create a culture where questioning is welcomed. SEL cannot be reduced to interpersonal skill-building or self-regulation strategies while leaving institutional power structures intact. Adult SEL requires an unwavering commitment to justice, ensuring that the persistence of institutional oppression does not compromise the emotional well-being of staff and students (Huizar, Phillips, & Gorski, 2025).

## Origins of Social and Emotional Learning

Dr. James Comer, a Black child psychiatrist and professor at the Yale School of Medicine, knew belonging matters and that "no significant learning happens without significant relationships." His insights remain as relevant today as when he first articulated them. Comer led research highlighting the role of non-academic factors in fostering children's well-being and academic achievement. His belief in collaboration among teachers, administrators, and parents to meet the holistic needs of students continues to be a model for effective education. Comer understood that context matters and individual well-being cannot be meaningfully addressed without tackling the institutional barriers that marginalize certain students. His vision incorporated a commitment to addressing institutional issues and meeting the needs of children.

Comer's work provided a foundation that inspired further developments in the field. By 1994, the Collaborative for Academic, Social, and Emotional Learning (CASEL) was established, reflecting growing awareness and efforts to ensure students' social and emotional growth is prioritized alongside their academic development. CASEL has been a leading organization that has brought SEL into schools and mainstream awareness. However, CASEL's most significant shortcoming is that it has never been clear that SEL does not exist without an explicit commitment to equity and justice.

SEL efforts often focus on helping individuals manage emotions without addressing how students with marginalized identities experience bias and discrimination. When SEL prioritizes harmony over justice, it can deepen harm rather than reduce it. Teaching students to "get along" without acknowledging power dynamics, such as how a Black, Muslim, or trans student might face microaggressions, fails to address systemic inequities (Simmons, 2021).

For SEL to be effective, it must confront disparities, ensuring all students feel seen, supported, and empowered to navigate their emotions and talk about the inequities they face. This is where CASEL's approach and the field of SEL must evolve by making equity and justice central. Research shows that SEL is most effective when explicitly addressing identity, agency, and justice rather than focusing solely on individual skill-building (Jagers, Rivas-Drake, & Williams, 2019). Equity cannot be an optional add-on to SEL; it must be its foundation. Otherwise, SEL risks reinforcing privilege rather than dismantling systemic barriers.

## Schools must be communities of belonging

Following in the footsteps of Comer, researchers have studied the relationship between a student's sense of belonging and its impact on psychological well-being and motivation. Carol Goodenow and Kathleen Grady defined school belonging as a student's sense of being "personally accepted, respected, included, and supported by others—especially teachers and other adults in the school social environment" (Goodenow & Grady, 1993). Dena Simmons (2021) described communities of belonging as ones where "all people, including the staff and the faculty, have the privilege and the safety to learn and live in the comfort of their skin."

Student belonging has been tied to academic achievement, reduced feelings of alienation and isolation, improved mental health, and lower risk of anxiety and depression. It has even been tied to emotional stability, joyful learning experiences, and increased happiness. However, many young people do not feel they belong in schools, do not feel personally accepted or respected, do not experience joy in school learning, are unhappy at school, and do not have the privilege and safety of learning in the comfort of their skin.

Consider how these policies and practices directly undermine student belonging:

**Book Bans and Curriculum Censorship.** School districts in more than 30 states have passed or proposed laws banning books and restricting how educators can teach about race, gender identity, and LGBTQ+ topics. In some districts, teachers are told to remove classroom libraries or avoid using words like "racism" or "inequity." Materials that reflect the experiences of students of color, LGBTQ+ students, and immigrant communities are often the first to be removed. Palestinian perspectives have also been targeted, with educators having faced discipline for including Palestinian voices in the curriculum and students having been told not to mention Gaza or Palestine, even in relevant academic contexts.

**Anti-LGBTQ+ Student Policies.** Several states now have laws that prevent transgender students from using bathrooms or participating in sports aligned with their gender identity. In some districts, educators are required to report any student who uses a different name or pronouns to their parents. These policies insert adults into students' private identities and reduce students' autonomy over how they show up at school.

**Disproportionate Discipline, Corporal Punishment, and School Policing.** Black students are consistently suspended, expelled, and referred to law enforcement at higher rates than white students for the same behaviors. Subjective violations like "defiance" or "disrespect" are more likely to result in punishment when applied to Black students. Corporal punishment remains legal in 17 states. At the same time, schools serving predominantly Black, Brown, and low-income students are more likely to rely on School Resource Officers, random searches, and metal detectors while lacking access to counselors and mental health professionals. This over-policing of students feeds a well-documented school-to-prison pipeline, pushing students out of classrooms and into contact with the criminal justice system.

**Language Restrictions and Bias Toward Multilingual Learners.** In some states, English-only laws block bilingual instruction entirely. Schools often prioritize English acquisition over content mastery or cultural connection even where bilingual education is allowed. Multilingual learners are frequently isolated in separate classrooms and given low-level work. Families who don't speak English fluently often receive limited, delayed, or inaccessible school communication.

**Islamophobia in Schools.** Muslim students often experience scrutiny, harassment, and disciplinary action in school settings. In some cases, students have been blocked from praying during the school day, questioned or ridiculed about their attire, or denied halal meal options. Requests for religious accommodations, such as prayer space or flexibility during Ramadan, are often dismissed or ignored.

The students who most often feel they don't belong are those whose identities are marginalized, usually not by accident. This results from institutional policies and everyday practices like the ones just named. So, how are we actively changing those conditions to ensure every student feels seen, valued, and included?

## Is SEL the answer?

If you think I'm going to say social and emotional learning is the answer, I'm not, and it isn't. At least not how I've seen it done in schools. It *could be* a meaningful part of the answer. I say part because it was never designed to fix institutional and systemic inequities that impede belonging. But I wholeheartedly believe that if we, the adults, can use SEL to change ourselves, we can change some of the practices in the institutions we work within with our eyes toward equity and belonging. That is what this book is about.

Most educators I've met care about young people and want to create communities where they belong and thrive. However, the institutions we work within and how we have been conditioned to behave within them lead us to create or uphold conditions that impede our belonging. For example, I have consulted in schools where teachers punish Black students in schools that have no dress codes for wearing hoodies, claiming the students are "disrespectful," or shaming girls for wearing spaghetti straps and "distracting the boys." I have worked with administrators who are afraid to address this kind of teacher behavior for fear they will be reported to the superintendent or discussed at a school board meeting. I have worked with teachers who have been reprimanded for expressing concerns that a mandated reading curriculum lacks relevant texts for the students they teach. In many schools, the culture dissuades honest and hard feedback and even punishes people for naming how we harm each other and students.

Often, we try to mitigate students' absence of belonging through social and emotional learning initiatives. We use SEL as the solution to help students fit in and belong because we presume we, the adults, have social and emotional competence, but our students don't.

When we do this, we assign young people the responsibility of developing the skillsets, mindsets, and behaviors to help them experience school belonging. We offer to teach them social and emotional skills to support this development. For example, we may teach them mindfulness practices to help them stay focused and calm. We might utilize team-building games and exercises so they form closer relationships and feel a greater sense of connection. We teach restorative approaches so that when they have conflicts, they can resolve them. But we also continue to utilize punitive practices, like demerit systems, insisting that they "track us when we speak," or kicking students out of the classroom when they talk out of turn too many times or won't begin their assignment when we tell them to. We get frustrated when these SEL approaches do not work or are insufficient.

These approaches don't work and aren't enough because they don't address the root issues that impede belonging: institutional inequity and implicit bias; in fact, they often uphold institutional inequities and reinforce our implicit biases. We repeatedly use SEL to get students who are most likely to experience injustice to self-manage and regulate their emotions in ways that meet our expectations rather than helping them authentically interpret and process their emotions so that they can engage with their school communities in healthy and just ways.

Take Briana, a Black, bubbly fourth-grader bussed from a low-income city neighborhood to an affluent, predominantly white suburban school. Briana navigated a world where some adults treated her presence as an anomaly. Teachers at her school opened the days with morning meetings, each ending with a mindfulness session, reminding students to close their eyes, breathe deeply, and "let go of distractions and be ready for the day." However, Briana's distractions occurred when teachers corrected her speech, made offhanded remarks about her neighborhood, or told her she was "too loud." Her teachers did not recognize that she experienced alienation as one of the few Black students at her school due to a state-funded school desegregation program. Rather than fostering a genuine sense of belonging, the focus remained on compliance and fitting in, leaving Briana to navigate her emotions in what often felt like an often unwelcoming environment.

*Institutional inequity* refers to the systematic unfairness or disparities built into educational institutions' structures, policies, practices, and procedures. Some examples that most of us are aware of are funding disparities, tracking, access to AP courses, discipline disparities, and overrepresentation in special education.

For example, institutional racism is visible in the education system, and we can see it in the unequal opportunities tied to race and socioeconomic status. Schools in low-income, predominantly Black or Brown neighborhoods typically receive less funding than schools in wealthier, mostly white areas.

Then there are the more subtle policies that are "just the way we do things" or embedded in the school's "culture," like charging families for field trips or sports participation, or grading homework. Students from families with fewer resources may lack access to study spaces, technology, or the internet, hindering their ability to complete assignments. Additionally, obligations such as part-time jobs or caring for younger siblings can limit the time available for homework.

Even dress codes, often framed as neutral, are enforced in ways that disproportionately target students of color, low-income students, and gender nonconforming students. For example, students may be disciplined for hairstyles, head coverings, or clothing that reflect their racial, cultural, or gender identities. These policies result in unequal opportunities, treatment, and outcomes based on race, ethnicity, socioeconomic status, gender, ability, or other marginalized identities, exacerbating disparities that already exist.

*Implicit bias* refers to unconscious attitudes, beliefs, stereotypes, or prejudices that influence our perceptions, decisions, and interactions. These biases are automatic and outside of conscious awareness. They shape our behaviors and contribute to unequal treatment or opportunities for students based on factors such as race, ethnicity, gender, and socioeconomic status. Implicit biases manifest in behaviors that favor "normativity"— socially constructed norms, values, and expectations that dictate how individuals behave, present themselves, and interact within a particular setting. Normativity involves reinforcing cultural norms and standards that privilege certain groups while marginalizing or excluding other groups. In the United States and its schools, we privilege whiteness, adultness, maleness, cisgenderness, heterosexuality, able-bodiedness, slim-bodiedness, athleticism, Christianity, and neurotypicality.

For example, in the U.S. and its schools, whiteness is often privileged through curriculum and representation. History and literature classes frequently emphasize the experiences and contributions of white people, often omitting the stories of Black, Indigenous, and other people of color. White students also experience fewer disciplinary actions than students of color for the same behaviors.

Adultness is privileged by centering authority, decision-making, and perspectives around adults rather than students. Policies, rules, and even teaching methods are designed without input from students, even though these policies, rules, and methods directly impact them. Adults hold the power to make decisions about what is taught, how it's taught, and how discipline is enforced, often dismissing student voices. This normativity leads to different expectations for students, exclusionary practices, and subtle (or not-so-subtle) forms of favoritism. I would be remiss if I did not say that, as a white woman, I grapple with my responsibility and complicity in the institutional inequities and implicit biases I am writing about.

## SEL is Our Work as Leaders

As leaders, we either clear the path for equity-centered change or stand in its way. Equity-centered change requires us to confront inequities head-on, and to do that, we must have a deep commitment to confronting biases, cultivating social and emotional competencies, and examining the institutional structures perpetuating inequity.

It starts with us. We cannot delegate, script, or layer equity in SEL on top of what we already do. It lives in how we lead, relate, and respond when things get hard.

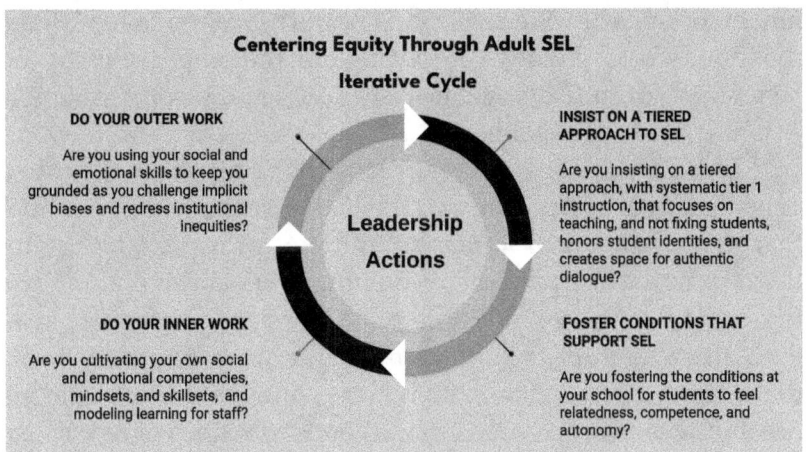

**FIGURE 0.1** Centering Equity Through Adult SEL Iterative Cycle

I believe there are four main aspects of centering equity in SEL, illustrated in this iterative change cycle:

Some of us have engaged with parts of this cycle, and some might not have engaged with any of them. All four components of an equity-centered SEL change cycle are essential. In Chapter 1, we will explore a tiered approach to SEL, and the importance of systematic tier 1 instruction that focuses on teaching and not fixing students, honors student identities, and creates space for authentic dialogue. In Chapter 2, we'll explore conditions that support SEL, including relatedness, competence, and autonomy. However, the heart of this book is about doing the *inner work of SEL* to do *the outer work of equity and justice*. In Chapters 3–8, I will share a collection of practices I have used and continue to use for my personal development and that I regularly teach to adults in workshops and 1:1 coaching. When applied with consistency, care, and commitment, these practices can change us, and then we can change the institutions we work within.

## We Each Need to do Our Inner Work

To truly embrace social and emotional learning, we need to be on a lifelong journey of self-discovery and growth, exploring the inner workings of our emotions. This journey, often called "doing the inner work," involves exploring our thoughts, feelings, and behaviors to cultivate greater self-awareness, self-regulation, empathy, and social skills.

"Doing the inner work" is crucial for equity work because it helps us uncover and confront the biases, fears, and insecurities that shape our actions, often without our awareness. It requires us to examine the patterns of our thoughts and emotions and understand how they influence our actions and interactions with each other. In equity work, we may enter into it with the belief that we must confront our own biases and institutional inequities, but when we are questioned about our actions or face resistance, when we're required to step outside of our comfort zones, we don't do it.

Particularly for those of us who are white and, to a large degree, have been entitled to comfort, we need to prepare ourselves for the fact that equity work will require us to confront our insecurities, self-doubt, and fears. By understanding how our emotions influence our reactions, especially when we face resistance or discomfort, we can prepare ourselves to respond thoughtfully rather than impulsively. This makes us better equipped to stay engaged in and committed to the work, to manage difficult conversations about race, privilege, and injustice, and to support colleagues on their journeys of growth.

This inner work isn't a one-time event. It's ongoing and foundational to the success of our outer work in equity.

## We Each Need to do Outer Work

We consider the conditions (the policies, practices, cultural norms) we create and uphold in our school, which either support or undermine student belonging. Moreover, when we consider these conditions, we do so through the lens of the student experience. We think about how students with marginalized identities experience these conditions and *institute changes that redress the inequities* they experience, leading to conditions that foster belonging and result in authentic social and emotional learning and growth.

"Outer work" is centered on applying what we learn from our inner work to create real change in our school communities. It is where we demonstrate our commitment to equity through the changes we make in our schools and classrooms.

It requires us to actively challenge inequitable systems and practices in our schools, from how discipline is handled to who has access to advanced courses. This means evaluating the curriculum, teaching methods, policies, practices, and cultural norms that disadvantage marginalized students. Doing this outer work means moving beyond intention into action—addressing disparities in discipline, ensuring all students have access to opportunities, and creating spaces where every student feels seen, heard, and valued.

This book is not a set of guidelines but an invitation to begin or deepen a journey toward equity-centered change. To do this work, we are called to look inward, to confront and cultivate our social and emotional capacities, and to recognize the essential connection between our inner development and the equitable, compassionate environments we strive to create. Reflect on how each chapter resonates with your personal and professional experiences. Each chapter will offer practical tools and strategies to consistently engage with inner and outer work, knowing that they lay the foundation for meaningful, equity-centered leadership. Through this process, I hope we can all become leaders who foster spaces where every student—and every educator—can grow, belong, and thrive.

# Part 1
## Foundations of SEL

# 1

# A Tiered Approach Starts with All Students in Mind

**Big Ideas in This Chapter**

- SEL must be universal and embedded into daily instruction. When SEL is reserved for certain students or used only in moments of crisis, it reinforces stigma and misses its purpose. Every student deserves consistent, integrated SEL that supports growth and belonging.
- SEL must confront white normativity. Practices rooted in individualism, emotional control, and compliance often marginalize students whose cultural expressions and lived experiences differ from dominant norms.
- Authentic SEL is embodied, inclusive, and relational. It should support students in naming and expressing emotions, connecting with others, and understanding how their identities and experiences shape their movement through the world.
- Educators need space to engage with SEL themselves. For SEL to serve students well, adults must reflect on their own social-emotional development and receive meaningful professional learning grounded in equity.

What if the framework designed to support students' emotional growth and well-being reinforces exclusion instead? What if the dominant cultural norms embedded in schools skew our understanding of Social and Emotional Learning (SEL) in ways we don't always recognize? In this chapter, we'll examine how cultural norms, particularly white normativity, can shape and distort the implementation of SEL. Even with the best intentions, these norms can lead to practices that perpetuate othering rather than fostering truly inclusive and authentic learning environments. This challenge is especially critical when developing a Tier 1 approach, where SEL should be integrated into daily instruction for all students, rather than reserved as an intervention for select groups at Tiers 2 and 3.

We'll explore how SEL can be intentionally woven into the fabric of every classroom and learning experience, ensuring that it is present and equitably accessible to all students. We'll reflect on where SEL currently "lives" in your school or district and how to ensure it serves every student, not just those who fit within dominant cultural expectations.

## Case Study: Breathing Away Your Troubles

An SEL practitioner shared the story of his work at The Neighborhood School, where students practiced a self-management technique to cultivate cognitive control, emphasizing its role in maintaining focus on long-term goals and ignoring distractions. He referenced an international study, which found that children who developed better cognitive control early on were healthier and wealthier in their thirties, more so than their peers with higher IQs or from wealthier families.

The students were taught a breathing exercise involving a stuffed animal to strengthen cognitive control. They lay down and placed a stuffed animal on their belly. They breathed in through their noses for a count of three while watching the stuffed animal rise. Then, they breathed out for three, watching the stuffed animal lower.

He claimed that this technique has been particularly effective in what he described as tough environments such as this one, where students are "dirt poor, live in housing projects, are traumatized, and many have ADHD." While his experience told him that schools like this were often chaotic, he believed that the class was calm and focused thanks to exercises like this.

Does your school implement activities like this one? If so, what is the goal of such an activity? What assumptions or beliefs about students do you have that led you to adopt such a practice? Later in this chapter, we'll revisit this scenario and explore how normativity can impede our good intentions.

## What SEL Is

Where does SEL live in your school or district? Does your school have a "school culture team" that manages discipline and SEL? Is SEL paired with special education services? Is SEL the responsibility of counselors and social workers? Too often, how we perceive and implement SEL reflects a fundamental misunderstanding, delegating it outside the core instructional experience that all students deserve. SEL is frequently misconstrued as a remedy for students dealing with trauma, learning disabilities, and behavior issues or as a means of managing emotional or disciplinary problems. SEL is often used primarily with "difficult students" because many educators view social-emotional learning as a tool to manage behavior rather than as a universal approach for all students. In these cases, SEL becomes a means to address specific challenges, such as defiance or disengagement, rather than fostering social and emotional competencies across the entire student population. This narrow application can reinforce the misconception that SEL is only for students who need behavioral correction rather than a foundational part of learning for everyone.

When we ask, "Where does SEL live in your school or district?" it's crucial to recognize that the answer should be "everywhere." Many of us turn to the CASEL Wheel, one of the most widely recognized frameworks, which outlines SEL's five core competencies:

- Self-awareness
- Self-management
- Social awareness
- Relationship skills
- Responsible decision-making

CASEL defines SEL as "...the process through which all young people and adults acquire and apply the knowledge, skills, and attitudes to develop healthy identities, manage emotions and achieve personal and collective goals, feel and show empathy for others, establish and maintain supportive relationships, and make responsible and caring decisions" (CASEL, 2020). This definition underscores that SEL is a process, not just a set of skills taught in response to specific challenges. It's not a one-time lesson or an isolated curriculum. It's a dynamic, evolving process that all students and adults must engage with, shaping how we learn, relate to each other, and navigate the world around us.

As educators, we know that teaching any process requires more than simply understanding its definition. For example, we know what reading is. However, students need systematic instruction to learn to read proficiently, and educators need more tools and training to teach it effectively, especially as students have diverse learning needs. The same is true for SEL. We must understand the "process through which all young people and adults acquire" the knowledge, skills, and attitudes associated with SEL, and we must understand how to teach that process in ways that resonate with different learners in different contexts.

Without intentional integration, SEL often remains fragmented, with limited impact. When SEL is treated as an add-on rather than embedded into daily instruction, it frequently fails to become sustainable or equitable (Jones et al., 2021). Schools must ensure that SEL is not just an occasional lesson or the responsibility of specialists but is woven into the fabric of every classroom, just like literacy and numeracy. SEL should be an integral part of the daily experience for all students, embedded in every aspect of school life, not just reserved for when things go wrong. When SEL is integrated into the core curriculum, it becomes an integral part of the school community's fabric. It shifts from an "intervention" to a cornerstone of a positive, inclusive learning environment where students can thrive.

## What SEL Isn't: Common Misconceptions in Social and Emotional Learning

One of the most evident signs that we've misunderstood SEL is when we assign it to specific teams or roles, such as discipline teams, special education departments, or school counselors, who handle particular problems or "difficult" students. This approach reduces SEL to an intervention rather than the fundamental instructional experience that all students need and deserve.

Perhaps this misunderstanding stems from the neglect of the word "all" in CASEL's definition, which is critical to SEL's purpose. SEL is for everyone. It isn't just for students from disadvantaged backgrounds or those struggling with trauma, ADHD, or anxiety. It is not a behavior management strategy or an approach to discipline or special education. It isn't designed as an intervention for students who struggle to "fit in." It isn't a tool to manage behavior in Black and Brown students or a strategy for students from low-income communities to deal with poverty.

When we fail to apply SEL universally, we risk reinforcing existing inequities. Traditional SEL models often overlook students' sociopolitical realities (Jagers, Rivas-Drake, & Borowski, 2018). If SEL is applied without an equity lens, it can perpetuate harm rather than address and disrupt inequities. SEL must explicitly consider students' cultural and social contexts rather than treating SEL as a neutral or decontextualized skill set.

SEL is sometimes misused as a tool for compliance rather than as a means of empowerment. Reducing SEL to behavior management reinforces racial and socioeconomic educational disparities (Simmons, 2021). Instead of fostering emotional intelligence and self-awareness, SEL can be weaponized to demand "self-regulation" from students without addressing the systemic conditions that shape their school experiences. This approach disproportionately impacts marginalized students, especially students of color, who are often expected to "control their emotions" in ways that align with dominant cultural norms.

When designed and implemented thoughtfully, SEL can support every identity in the school ecosystem. It should not be used as a mechanism for social control but as a tool to create learning environments where every student can engage authentically. By embedding SEL across the curriculum and ensuring it is taught with an equity-centered approach, schools can foster communities where students feel seen, valued, and empowered.

| Misunderstandings in common practices *When SEL is misunderstood, we might see examples like the following.* ||
|---|---|
| **SEL Reserved for "At-Risk" Students Only** | In many schools, SEL programs are only offered to students labeled "at-risk" or having been identified with behavior problems. These students might be placed in small groups to focus on emotional regulation, managing anger, or dealing with trauma. This approach creates a false divide between those deemed to need social-emotional support and those assumed to have it figured out. Students from marginalized groups are stigmatized as being in greater need of emotional or behavioral "correction." |
| **SEL in Discipline, but Not in the Classroom** | In some schools, SEL practices are used when addressing discipline issues. Students who disrupt class or break school rules are sent to a counselor, where they are taught skills like self-regulation, conflict resolution, or mindfulness to "correct" their behavior. They encounter SEL in reactive situations when they are already in trouble. This reinforces the idea that SEL is not a foundational part of every student's daily learning experience but a tool for "fixing" behavior issues. |
| **SEL Programs that Don't Reflect Students' Experiences** | Many SEL programs are designed around values and behaviors rooted in white, middle-class cultural norms, such as individual achievement, compliance, and emotional regulation. For example, a school might introduce SEL lessons that focus on "grit" or "perseverance," concepts that place the onus on students to work harder and overcome obstacles through personal effort. They can disregard barriers like xenophobia, racism, or poverty that marginalized students may face. |

| Misunderstandings in common practices<br>*When SEL is misunderstood, we might see examples like the following.* ||
|---|---|
| **Lack of SEL for Adults in the School Community** | In most schools, SEL is entirely student-focused, with no emphasis on SEL for adults. This creates a disconnect where staff—teachers, administrators, and support personnel—are expected to teach and model SEL skills that they may not have developed or practiced. |

## A Tiered Approach Starts with Tier 1

For leaders, resisting using SEL as an intervention can feel tough. When teachers are struggling, aren't connecting with students, don't have effective classroom management strategies, or ask us to do more to help them, it can be tempting to use SEL to create some sense of order and control. But when SEL is at its best, we, the adults, have worked to cultivate it. It affords us the self-awareness, self-management, social awareness, and relationship skills to work toward authentic solutions to many of the inequities our students face, rather than merely applying a band-aid to a deeper issue.

To ensure SEL reaches *all* students, we must adopt a tiered approach that starts with robust, tier 1 instruction. Like any academic subject, tier 1 SEL instruction requires content expertise, a curriculum, a pedagogical approach, an implementation plan, and an effectiveness assessment.

| **Tiered Supports Framework Explained** (Adapted from Panorama Education's comprehensive guide on MTSS) |
|---|
| MTSS stands for *Multi-Tiered System of Support*—a framework schools use to ensure every student gets what they need to succeed. It organizes support into three levels that increase in intensity depending on a student's needs. |
| **Tier 1: Universal Support** |
| These are the practices and supports that all students receive. High-quality instruction, embedded social-emotional learning, a positive and inclusive school climate, and consistent, caring classroom management are all part of Tier 1. The goal is to create strong, supportive environments that help most students thrive. |

| Tier 2: Targeted Support |
|---|
| When some students aren't progressing with Tier 1 alone, schools provide additional help through Tier 2 support. These are often small-group interventions focused on specific academic, behavioral, or social-emotional needs. Typically, 15–20% of students benefit from this extra layer. |
| **Tier 3: Intensive Support** |
| For the 1–5% of students who need more, Tier 3 offers individualized, intensive support. These services are tailored to address persistent or complex challenges and may involve specialists or more frequent one-on-one interventions. |

Tier 1 SEL instruction is crucial for ensuring that all students receive high-quality teaching and learning experiences, with access that supports the diverse needs of learners, regardless of their backgrounds, abilities, or current performance levels. By establishing a social-emotional foundation, Tier 1 SEL instruction helps students develop essential skills and knowledge. Solid Tier 1 instruction also allows for more efficient use of resources, as effective core instruction can minimize the need for intensive interventions. Additionally, it encourages collaboration among educators, families, and the community, enhancing the educational experience for all students. To ensure that SEL is Tier 1, meaning it is universally available to all students as part of the core curriculum, here are several foundational criteria to consider:

**Provide Direct Instruction on SEL skills.** This can include teaching emotional awareness, problem-solving, and conflict resolution through structured lessons or programs. For example, we could teach emotional literacy by introducing an emotions wheel and instructing students on how to transition from general emotions, such as sadness, to more specific ones, like disappointment or discouragement.

**Integrate SEL into the Academic Curriculum.** Embed SEL competencies into academic subjects, using opportunities within lessons to teach skills like self-awareness, empathy, and relationship building. For example, we could prepare students to invite peers to be their discussion partners in a reading classroom and teach them about the emotional impact of being included.

**Create Opportunities for Practice.** Design activities that allow students to practice SEL skills, such as cooperative learning, peer mentoring, and community service projects. In group work, for example, students might be tasked with completing a project, assigning roles, making collaborative decisions, and resolving disagreements. We might set specific checkpoints where the group reflects on how they worked together, what emotional challenges arose, and how they might revise the process next time.

**Model SEL Skills in Interactions with Students and Other Adults.** For example, a teacher might say, "I can see you're frustrated. Let's take a minute to breathe, and then let's talk through it together. I want to hear what's going on for you and understand how I can help." This shows how to handle emotions constructively and practice active listening.

**Use Regular Assessments and Feedback.** Utilize tools such as student surveys or assessments to evaluate the effectiveness of SEL initiatives and make necessary adjustments. This feedback loop can help refine strategies and ensure all students benefit. For example, a school could use a simple survey asking students to rate how safe, supported, and understood they feel at school. The results help teachers adjust their SEL strategies to better meet student needs.

**Provide Ongoing Training** for educators to equip them with the skills and knowledge necessary to implement SEL effectively. This begins with ensuring the staff develops an ongoing practice for their own social and emotional development.

These criteria may sound familiar because they are nearly identical to our considerations when implementing a tier 1 reading curriculum. As we would in reading, we should use evidence-based SEL programs designed for universal implementation, ensuring they align with the school community's needs and culture. By using these strategies, schools can ensure that SEL is an integral part of the educational experience for all students.

## Effective Tier 1 Requires Addressing White Normativity in SEL

Although SEL is often framed as neutral, many SEL frameworks and practices reflect white cultural norms. While Dr. James Comer, a Black educator, laid the foundation for SEL work, white researchers and reformers shaped much of the modern discourse. This has led to SEL practices that center on white norms and ignore the cultural experiences of Black, Brown, Indigenous, and other students of color.

"White normativity" refers to the assumption that white cultural values, beliefs, behaviors, and aesthetics are the default, ideal, or neutral standards by which all other racial identities or ethnicities are measured. By normalizing whiteness and rendering other cultural perspectives and experiences less visible, less valid, or less important, white normativity contributes to the marginalization of many of our students' identities.

In educational settings, white normativity can appear in curricula that predominantly feature white historical figures, characters, and authors; teaching methods that reflect white cultural expectations; dress codes that replicate the dress of business casual white men; or discipline policies that disproportionately affect students of color. Recognizing and disrupting white normativity is essential to advancing equity because it is directly connected to deficit-based thinking when students, or even colleagues, don't fit with white norms.

White normativity in SEL often manifests through emphasizing individualism, emotional regulation, and compliance. It prioritizes self-control, grit, resilience, and a growth mindset, linking SEL to academic achievement and workforce readiness in ways that disregard students navigating institutional and systemic barriers beyond their control.

When SEL is practiced through the lens of white normativity, it sends a harmful message to students of color that their identities, lived experiences, and cultural backgrounds are not valued. Dena Simmons, founder of LiberatED, an organization dedicated to racial justice in social and emotional learning, emphasizes that the ability to discuss SEL without addressing identity is itself a reflection of white privilege. "You can't have those conversations without talking about identity… Social-emotional learning is so that people can get along better. We also have to discuss why people don't get along," she explains. Without an explicitly anti-racist, abolitionist, and anti-oppressive approach, she warns, SEL risks becoming little more than "white supremacy with a hug" (Simmons, 2019).

Consider the Neighborhood School and the mindful breathing exercise mentioned earlier. Mindfulness itself isn't the problem. It's a practice with deep roots in Buddhist tradition, and it can be a powerful tool for emotional awareness and regulation. The issue lies in how it is interpreted and applied in school settings. Stillness and quiet aren't the only, or even the best, indicators of emotional regulation. When schools treat calm as the standard for success, they risk overlooking the emotional complexity of students who express themselves differently. In particular, behaviors like movement, vocal expression, or assertiveness are often interpreted as dysregulation or disrespect in Black and Brown students. In contrast, the same behaviors may be overlooked or reinterpreted when exhibited by white students. Emotional regulation is about helping students understand and manage their feelings in ways that are developmentally appropriate, culturally responsive, and grounded in genuine connection, rather than just outward behavior.

Mindful breathing can support calmness and focus. While research with children is still in development, some evidence suggests that it can aid in the development of self-regulation and attention (van de Weijer-Bergsma, 2024). For some students, it may be a helpful tool, before a test, after a frustrating interaction, or when preparing for a high-pressure moment, such as a spelling bee or a big game. However, it's essential not to overstate its impact or treat it as a universal solution. A few minutes of breathing won't resolve systemic issues like discipline disparities or inequitable access to support. Mindfulness might be more appropriately directed at the adults in the building, those whose bias-informed emotional reactions often shape how student behavior is interpreted and disciplined. When used thoughtfully, mindfulness can help adults pause, reflect, and interrupt reactive patterns that contribute to inequitable outcomes.

But mindful breathing doesn't solve poverty, curricular erasure, or discipline practices that disproportionately impact marginalized students (Losen & Jordan, 2021). If we fail to address the structural barriers that students, for example, living in poverty face, these sorts of exercises, absent a commitment to equity and justice, risk becoming another way to ask students to cope with inequity rather than challenge it.

For SEL to truly serve all students, it must move beyond symptomatic solution-level techniques and engage deeply with the cultural, racial, and social realities that shape students' lives. We must always be prepared to examine whose norms are being centered and who benefits from these practices, ensuring that SEL is a tool that is meaningful to everyone and fosters genuine belonging for every student.

## The Problem with Individualism in SEL

Individualism, a hallmark of many white-normed SEL practices, is often emphasized through grit, growth mindset, and resilience. These ideas can be beneficial when applied thoughtfully, but they become problematic when they dominate SEL discourse, particularly in ways that fail to acknowledge the many students with marginalized identities.

Consider Jem, a student praised for her "grit" and determination. She lives in a neighborhood with limited resources, where her family faces economic hardships. Teachers frequently use Jem as an example of individual resilience, pointing out how she excels and reinforcing the belief that excelling is a choice some students make while others don't.

By framing Jem's success solely as the result of individual effort, the school sends the message that success is simply a matter of personal perseverance and that the other students must demonstrate the same grit to achieve similar results. By placing the burden of success on individual effort, SEL practices that focus on individualism overlook the role of privilege and inequities that shape students' opportunities for success.

We must also incorporate approaches prioritizing relationships and collective problem-solving to counteract this.

There are many ways to do this, including creating consistent opportunities for students to connect through structured peer discussions, integrating role-playing activities that help students understand different perspectives, or collective problem-solving through collaborative projects where students work together to address real-world challenges.

Imagine that Jem's teacher notices frequent student complaints about the short recess time. These students often discuss the need for more time to unwind and play. The teacher facilitates a collective problem-solving discussion rather than dismissing the complaints or expecting students to cope on their own.

She engages with the students by asking them open-ended questions, such as "Why do you think recess is important for us?" and "What impact would a longer recess have on our school day?" These questions encourage students to think beyond their individual experiences and consider the broader benefits or challenges of a longer recess. The teacher then guides them to work in small groups to brainstorm potential solutions, asking them to consider how they could present their case to the administration and anticipate the challenges that might arise, such as how a longer recess might impact instructional time.

Jem and her classmates come up with ideas, such as gathering research on how longer recess improves focus and behavior, interviewing students and teachers to gather different perspectives, and creating a proposal with a schedule adjustment. Throughout the process, the teacher helps them refine their thinking, shows them how to collaborate and solve the problem collectively, and reinforces that they have the power to create change by working together.

These approaches help build interconnectedness and student voice and make SEL a shared experience rather than a targeted intervention. SEL can help build strong, interconnected communities where everyone has the support they need to thrive.

## Beyond Emotional Regulation: Embodied SEL

Another common issue with SEL is its overemphasis on emotional regulation, particularly for students. While managing emotions is important, SEL is too often framed as something we *do to* students, not *with* them, and rarely something adults are expected to practice themselves. This student-facing approach overlooks the embodied, relational nature of emotional experiences and ignores the systemic conditions that shape them. We maintain unjust systems when adults remain disconnected from themselves and others. True SEL attends to both mind and body, and must include adults, acknowledging how systemic injustices affect our physical and emotional well-being.

Somatic strategies such as breathwork or stress-release exercises can help students and adults engage with SEL holistically, moving beyond cognitive control to foster genuine well-being. In a middle school classroom, the teacher knows students often return from recess full of energy, exuberant, talkative, and restless. Rather than immediately beginning the lesson or asking them to sit quietly, she introduces a brief movement-based activity to help them settle.

She guides the class through simple exercises to release tension and bring awareness to their bodies. They start with deep, intentional breaths, focusing on slow inhalations and full exhalations. Next, she leads a "shake it out" exercise, encouraging students to shake their hands, arms, legs, and shoulders to dispel excess energy. To ground them further, she asks them to press their feet firmly into the floor, imagining roots anchoring them to the earth, while stretching their arms upward like branches reaching for the sky.

Through this practice, the teacher supports students in regulating their energy in a way that honors both their physical and emotional states. Rather than relying solely on cognitive strategies like urging them to "focus" or "calm down," she integrates the body's role in emotional balance. These somatic approaches give students a healthy, active way to release stress rather than suppressing it.

## Moving Away from Compliance and Control

Far too often in classrooms, SEL is used to promote compliance rather than empowerment. When emotional regulation is used to avoid confronting difficult emotions or to maintain calm at all costs, it stifles authentic expression and reinforces conformity to narrow emotional norms. In her book *The Color of Emotional Intelligence: Elevating Our Self and Social Awareness to Address Inequities*, Farah Harris explains, "Let's face it, even something as basic as chicken is prepared differently based on cultural or socioeconomic upbringing. If we can approach cooking differently, surely we can approach a skill like emotional intelligence in distinctive ways." But in schools, we usually don't. Instead, SEL is often framed through a dominant cultural lens that overlooks how social and emotional intelligence can and should manifest differently depending on a student's background and lived experiences.

This kind of regulation is particularly harmful to students of color, whose emotional experiences may be policed in ways that perpetuate stereotypes and contribute to disciplinary action. Research has found that Black students are more likely to be disciplined for subjective infractions like "disrespect" or "defiance." In contrast, similar behaviors from white students are often interpreted as expressions of passion or confidence (Darling-Hammond & Ho, 2024). These disparities stem from implicit biases that shape how teachers perceive and respond to students' emotions.

In a classroom where emotional regulation is framed as maintaining calm and composure at all costs, a teacher might interpret a Black student's frustration or assertiveness as disruptive or disrespectful, while a similar reaction from a white student might be seen as passion or stress. Imagine James, a Black student, who grows frustrated during a whole-class book discussion because he feels his perspective is being dismissed when a peer repeatedly interrupts him, despite the class practicing active listening, which James values. *"You keep cutting me off. How is this active listening?"* he asks pointedly. Instead of addressing the interruption, his teacher warns him that if he speaks out again, he will be removed from the discussion, treating the situation as a discipline issue rather than validating his frustration.

Rather than using SEL to enforce emotional conformity, schools must implement it in culturally responsive ways that affirm students' full range of emotions. Without this awareness, SEL risks becoming a tool for control rather than fostering self-awareness and empowerment.

Instead of policing James's emotions, a more responsive approach would be for the teacher to acknowledge his frustration, provide space for him to speak, and use the moment to reinforce what active listening looks and sounds like. Classrooms should encourage students to explore and express a full spectrum of emotions, fostering critical thinking and challenging practices that only serve some while silencing other students.

The table and figure below outline some typical ways white normativity appears in SEL practices, why it is problematic, and alternatives or additions to the approach. Consider your school's stance on these practices.

| Characteristic | How it shows up | Why is it problematic | Alternatives or additions |
|---|---|---|---|
| **Individualism** | Individualism manifests through subtle and direct messages to "pull yourself up by your bootstraps" and develop grit, a growth mindset, and resilience. It emphasizes perseverance, self-reliance, and academic achievement, linking social and emotional skills to improved academic performance and workforce readiness. | This mindset places an undue burden on students to overcome injustices and reinforces harmful stereotypes about their abilities and worth. It assumes success solely depends on individual effort and resilience, ignoring the role of privilege and systemic inequalities in shaping opportunities for success. It places an undue burden on individuals to overcome barriers beyond their control. | Community-oriented approaches that prioritize building a sense of belonging, interconnectedness, and collaboration within the learning community. These approaches emphasize circles, cooperative group projects, and community-building activities. These approaches allow students to practice addressing shared challenges and building supportive relationships in their classroom communities. |

| Characteristic | How it shows up | Why is it problematic | Alternatives or additions |
|---|---|---|---|
| **Emotional Regulation Instead of Embodied Approaches** | Emotional regulation and expression are taught or enforced without acknowledging cultural differences. There is often an overreliance on calmness and stillness, with strategies like mindfulness and breathing being popular tools. | It can become a tool of control, pushing students to adapt to white normative standards. Overlooks the embodied nature of emotional experiences. | Embodied SEL promotes a more holistic understanding of well-being by focusing on how emotions manifest in the body. It encourages students and adults to engage with their emotions in ways that honor both mind and body. This can lead to deeper emotional regulation, resilience, and authentic self-expression. Offer body-based strategies, such as attending to our bodies' overall well-being (food, sleep, movement, connection), or somatic strategies, such as breathwork, humming, vagal tone, or stress discharge exercises. |
| **Compliance and Control** | Compliance and control emphasize conformity to established norms and expectations, often prioritizing obedience over critical thinking. Students are expected to adapt their behavior and emotions to fit within existing power structures rather than challenging inequities or injustices. | This approach perpetuates a culture of passivity and acquiescence, discouraging students from questioning authority or advocating for change. Educators reinforce oppressive dynamics by prioritizing obedience over agency, inhibiting meaningful engagement. | Encourage students to question norms and advocate for social justice. Educators can cultivate a culture of empowerment and collective action within the learning community by fostering critical thinking skills and group problem solving. |

## Final Thoughts

Tier 1 SEL practices are essential for creating a foundation of emotional and social well-being for all students. Still, they must also be examined to determine how cultural norms, particularly white normativity, can shape their implementation. When SEL is embedded into everyday classroom experiences without challenging dominant norms, it can reinforce exclusion and othering. Schools must intentionally design SEL practices that honor a diversity of emotional expressions and avoid centering on one dominant cultural narrative. By doing so, SEL can become a tool for authentic belonging for all students, not just those who conform to normative expectations.

### *Bringing it Back to You*
- How do your personal experiences and identity shape the way you view and engage with SEL?
- Is SEL, in your view, currently being used more to support student growth or to manage student behavior, and how do you feel about that?
- Where have you seen SEL uphold dominant cultural norms, and how have you responded?
- What discomfort, if any, do you feel when students express strong emotions? How do you interpret and navigate those moments?
- What kind of learning or unlearning might you need to ensure your SEL practices are both effective and equity-centered?

### *Bringing it Back to Your Team*
- Where does SEL "live" in our school or district? Who is responsible for it, and where is it visible?
- How are we fostering a culture of student empowerment through SEL rather than reinforcing control or compliance as a team?

- What patterns or gaps do we notice in implementing SEL across different classrooms, grade levels, or student groups?
- What systems or structures are in place to help educators integrate SEL meaningfully into everyday teaching?
- How do we currently evaluate the impact of our SEL work, and how can we ensure that our measures align with the goals of equity, inclusion, and belonging?

# 2

# Creating the Conditions That Support SEL

> **Big Ideas in This Chapter**
>
> ♦ Students thrive when learning conditions support connection, capability, and choice. When classrooms foster relatedness, competence, and autonomy, students are more likely to feel motivated, engaged, and seen.
> ♦ SEL must be grounded in students' lived experiences. When programs ignore cultural, racial, and socioeconomic realities, they risk reinforcing exclusion and missing the needs of those most often marginalized.
> ♦ Deficit thinking undermines student potential. Assumptions about readiness, effort, or ability—especially for students with marginalized identities—reinforce inequities and limit opportunities to grow.
> ♦ Equity-centered SEL requires systemic awareness and adult reflection. Creating supportive conditions means addressing structural barriers, affirming identities, and examining how our own beliefs, power, and privilege shape school culture.

In Chapter 1, we explored the importance of a Tier 1 approach to social and emotional learning (SEL) and the need to check it for white normativity. But what happens when staff don't recognize their normative lens? Have you ever observed Tier 1 SEL instruction where students appear ritually compliant but disengaged or where student-teacher relationships seem underdeveloped? These moments reveal that SEL is more than competencies that are taught. It is also the conditions in which students learn them.

In this chapter, we'll examine how learning conditions shape students' experiences of SEL, and how those conditions, in turn, are shaped by adults' own social and emotional capacities. Learning conditions, such as relationships, structures, and expectations, can either support or hinder students' ability to engage and thrive. They also help reduce racial and other educational inequities. Research indicates that students' perceptions of their learning environment have a significant impact on their motivation, engagement, and academic achievement. With this in mind, we'll explore how meeting students' fundamental needs of relatedness, competence, and autonomy can create the conditions that allow SEL to be genuinely effective.

## Gabriel and Bellflower Middle School: When Plans Fall Short

Gabriel is a seventh grader at Bellflower Middle School in Ridgeland, a mountain resort town known for its ski resorts, high-end homes, and stark economic divides. With a population of just over 16,000, the town has some of the highest and lowest incomes in the country. For decades, immigrants have come for job opportunities. Before Gabriel was born, his parents made the arduous journey from Tlaxcala, Mexico, in search of work. His father works in construction, and his mother is a housekeeper, reflecting a broader trend in the town: Mexican fathers working in labor-intensive industries while mothers clean homes or resorts. Teachers describe Gabriel as friendly, good-humored, and easygoing, though "not the hardest worker" and "below grade level in most subjects." Like many of his Mexican peers, he works after school to support his family, a reality that staff acknowledge but have not deeply considered.

Bellflower's district prides itself on fostering social and emotional well-being, promoting diversity, respect, and community. The district's SEL Coordinator, Sarah, moved to Ridgeland from California nearly 20 years ago, drawn by the mountain biking scene. She developed a passion for SEL through her mindfulness practice, which she credits for helping her focus and excel in bike competitions. Wanting students to have that same focus, she worked with her team to create a homegrown SEL curriculum centered on mindfulness, personal resilience, and a growth mindset.

To support implementation, teachers participated in communities of practice to learn mindfulness strategies and resilience-building tools, such as "Bounce Back Plans," designed to help students recover from setbacks. In class, teachers guided students through discussions on resilience, encouraging them to reflect on personal challenges, how they felt, how they responded, and what they learned. Students then used the Bounce Back framework to identify a problem, acknowledge their emotions, brainstorm solutions, select an actionable step, and incorporate a self-care strategy. They shared their plans with peers, normalizing the process of overcoming challenges.

Sarah also helped revise the school report card to align with the district's SEL vision, believing that "if something matters, we should grade it." The new SEL categories included:

- **Focus:** Paying attention, staying on task, and avoiding distractions. Assessed through behaviors like completing homework, following instructions, and coming prepared with a charged laptop.
- **Resilience:** Persevering through challenges with a positive attitude. Assessed through behaviors like retaking a test after a low grade or seeking help when struggling with a new topic.
- **Growth Mindset:** Believing abilities develop through effort and persistence. Assessed through behaviors like

asking questions, trying new strategies, and viewing mistakes as learning opportunities.

Despite these efforts, not all students have benefited from them. Gabriel, for example, has struggled to create a meaningful Bounce Back Plan. His SEL scores were low after the first marking period, mirroring his academic struggles. He remains easygoing, and staff are unsure why he isn't thriving. He's not the only one, and they are committed to figuring out what's missing.

Considering Gabriel's experience at Bellflower, what feels familiar to you? What do you notice about how the district's approach accounts for differences in student cultures, identities, and socioeconomic realities? How well do staff seem to understand Gabriel's experiences, and is there evidence that they are equipped to build authentic relationships with him, foster his sense of competence, and create meaningful opportunities for him to share his voice?

We'll return to this scenario throughout the chapter.

## Relatedness, Competence, and Autonomy: What Students Need, and Adults Must Foster

We can't expect students to develop socially, emotionally, or academically if they feel unwelcome, incompetent, and disempowered when they come to school. Too many students have precisely that experience every day in school. We tend not to recognize the habits we've built around establishing school-based practices rooted in anticipation of what students aren't ready for: work they aren't capable of, freedoms they can't manage, or relationships they can't build. We see this in how schools restrict independent learning opportunities until students prove they can sit still, withhold rich literacy experiences based on assumptions about readiness, or design discipline policies that preemptively limit students' choices rather than teach them how to navigate responsibility. There's no doubt that students with marginalized identities suffer the most from this kind of deficit ideology.

Numerous studies have confirmed that supportive learning conditions significantly enhance students' motivation, engagement, and academic success, while also improving their social and emotional outcomes. When students encounter environments that affirm their identities, foster a sense of community, and offer meaningful opportunities for student input, they are more likely to develop a deep sense of belonging and invest in their learning.

Affirming students' identities is a fundamental part of this process. It means ensuring that they see themselves reflected in the curriculum, classroom materials, and everyday interactions, not as an afterthought, but as a foundational element of their learning experience. A typical example is ensuring that read-alouds or books reflect students' identities, featuring stories with protagonists who look like them and share similar experiences. To affirm identities meaningfully, however, we must recognize and value students' cultural backgrounds, identities, languages, and lived experiences as assets, not deficits. Research indicates that identity-safe classrooms foster engagement and improve academic outcomes (Cohn-Vargas, Kahn &Epstein, 2020).

While there are numerous models of learning conditions, one particularly compelling framework comes from Self-Determination Theory. This theory emphasizes three fundamental psychological needs that drive motivation: relatedness, competence, and autonomy (Deci & Ryan, 2020). These needs are essential for fostering intrinsic motivation, which is key to personal growth and engagement in learning.

## Intrinsic vs. Extrinsic Motivation

Motivation influences how we engage with tasks and, ultimately, how we learn. Intrinsic motivation arises from within us. When we're involved in something that aligns with our interests, values, or sense of identity, we experience joy or fulfillment. Think of a time when you were so engrossed in an activity, like a hobby or a project, that you lost track of time. This is an example of a "flow" state, a feeling of intense involvement in a task that feels both challenging and achievable (Piefer et al., 2022). Intrinsically motivated students are likelier to feel connected to their work and each other, fostering a deeper sense of purpose.

On the other hand, extrinsic motivation comes from external factors such as rewards or the fear of punishment. This type of motivation is often embedded in systems like the stoplight approach, paychecks, or Positive Behavior Interventions and Supports (PBIS), where students are encouraged to act in specific ways due to incentives or consequences. While these systems may improve short-term compliance, research indicates that they often fail to promote long-term engagement, particularly when they overlook students' cultural contexts and psychological needs (Jagers, Rivas-Drake, & Williams, 2019).

External rewards, particularly when experienced as controlling, can reduce students' sense of autonomy and competence, two critical drivers of intrinsic motivation (Ryan & Deci, 2020). These systems can reinforce behavioral compliance over meaningful self-regulation. Moreover, punitive approaches may erode trust and dampen students' connection to school, disproportionately affecting students with marginalized identities (Darling-Hammond et al., 2020).

In contrast, intrinsic motivators, such as relevance, belonging, and emotional safety, are more likely to foster deep learning and sustained effort. Adults play a crucial role here. When educators model curiosity, agency, and emotional investment in their learning, they help create an environment where intrinsic motivation can thrive. This is especially crucial for creating equitable, student-centered learning environments.

## Creating Conditions for Intrinsic Motivation in the Classroom

For students to be intrinsically motivated, we must design environments that support their need for relatedness, competence, and autonomy. Here's how these can look in the classroom:

## 1 Relatedness: Fostering Connection and Belonging

Relatedness is the need to feel known, cared for, and connected to other people. This can begin with simple gestures, such as greeting students, inviting participation, and valuing their opinions. However, actual relatedness is built on a deeper understanding of students' personal and cultural identities. Students need to feel recognized as unique individuals, not just as students who fit into a standardized mold. To support students in feeling truly connected and seen, educators can take intentional steps to build a sense of relatedness in the classroom:

- Take time to get to know each student, not just academically, but personally as well.
- Regularly check in with students to ensure you build ongoing, meaningful connections.
- Celebrate students' academic and personal growth on a regular basis.
- Use lesson content that reflects students' cultural identities and experiences.
- Learn about your identity and how it might influence your student interactions.
- Provide opportunities for students to collaborate, helping them build relationships with one another.
- Teach conflict-resolution strategies and cultivate empathy in your classroom.
- Build trust by helping students manage their time and work.
- Involve families in the educational process through flexible events and consistent communication.

## 2 Competence: Building Skills and Confidence

Competence is the need to feel capable and effective in our abilities. This means ensuring students have the knowledge and tools to succeed in the classroom. This can be achieved by scaffolding complex tasks, giving students ample practice opportunities, and offering feedback that helps them improve. To foster a learning environment where students feel confident and capable, educators can intentionally nurture a sense of competence:

- Model behaviors and skills for students, showing them what success looks like.
- Encourage peer modeling, where students can teach each other and reinforce their skills.
- Allow time for reflection so students can process what they've learned and understand how to apply it.
- Use inclusive language and strategies that reflect diverse cultural backgrounds and experiences.
- Offer positive, actionable feedback that helps students build their skills.
- Provide rubrics and criteria lists so students understand how to meet expectations.
- Showcase high-quality examples of student work so that students have a clear vision of what they can achieve.

## 3  Autonomy: Empowering Students to Take Ownership

Autonomy refers to the need to have control over our actions and decisions. This means allowing students to choose how and when to complete tasks in the classroom. It's essential that students feel they can pursue work that aligns with their interests and values and that they have the opportunity to reflect on and take responsibility for their learning. To support students in developing a sense of ownership over their learning, educators can create conditions that promote autonomy:

- Provide students with opportunities to choose how they will demonstrate their learning.
- Offer a variety of options for academic and social activities, enabling students to express themselves in meaningful ways.
- Regularly allow students to set goals and plan for achieving them.
- Teach students how to give and receive feedback, supporting their growth in a collaborative environment.
- Involve students in co-constructing classroom agreements, ensuring they feel a sense of ownership in the learning environment.

- Discuss how community agreements support a positive classroom culture, and give students a say in revising them when necessary.
- Empower students to understand the consequences of their actions and be involved in setting expectations for their behavior.

To create an environment where students thrive, we must foster strong relationships, provide meaningful challenges, and offer them choices in their learning. When students feel connected, capable, and in control of their learning, they engage more, grow in confidence, and develop the skills they need for long-term success.

## Centering Student Realities and Challenging Our Own Assumptions

The Bellflower staff identified SEL practices they wanted students to learn, but hadn't considered the conditions in which students would learn them. A lens of white normativity shaped the SEL approach. Drawing on her experiences with competitive mountain biking, Sarah developed strategies to cultivate focus and resilience. While the curriculum resonated with the school's staff and many students, it wasn't designed with all students in mind.

Like many educators, Sarah's team had a specific idea of what it meant for a student to demonstrate a growth mindset, resilience, and focus. They likely envisioned a student who is grades-conscious, always prepared, regularly participates, and complies with expectations. However, these traits do not necessarily indicate genuine engagement, effort, or the ability to navigate and overcome challenges. Too often, students who don't fit this mold are seen as lacking motivation rather than facing real barriers to success.

I'm reminded of Adam, a 6th grader who once came to my office frustrated. He shared, "Everyone has said I don't work or I'm lazy since first grade. But I work ten times as hard, and my work still doesn't look as good as everyone else's. There's something wrong with me, and even my parents won't take me seriously." An evaluation revealed that Adam had attention deficit disorder and that his processing was slower than what was considered the "normal range." This revelation shifted how the adults in his life saw and supported him. No one would ever again assume he wasn't working hard enough.

However, many students are not like Adam because they don't have the opportunity to express their struggles or challenge the assumptions adults hold about them. In light of this, we must be careful not to make assumptions about their effort or potential. We must remain open, humble, and curious about the gaps in our understanding of our students. We must move away from assumptions about what students *can* and *can't* do and instead focus on learning about their unique needs and strengths.

## Next Steps for Bellflower

For schools like Bellflower, considering all the necessary changes to create the ideal learning environment can feel overwhelming. However, taking it step by step is key. By focusing on the principles of relatedness, competence, and autonomy, Sarah and her team began to recognize gaps in their approach and expand their awareness of Gabriel's reality.

The following questions helped guide their reflection process, allowing them to consider where to start and which practices to adjust. They chose students with marginalized identities, including Gabriel, to frame their discussions. When evaluating school practices, it was helpful to consider both guiding questions and key reflection questions to gain a well-rounded understanding of students' experiences.

**Guiding questions** focused on identifying specific actions: what is working, what needs improvement, and what changes could enhance students' sense of belonging, competence, and autonomy. These questions helped them analyze and refine their approaches. In contrast, **key reflection questions** centered on students' perspectives, providing insight into whether they feel connected, capable, and empowered. Using both types of questions, they tried to ensure that their school environments were genuinely responsive to students' needs.

## Relatedness

*Guiding Questions:*

- ◆ What practices have we implemented that make students feel connected to the school community?
- ◆ What future practices will strengthen students' sense of belonging?
- ◆ What practices are hindering students from feeling connected?

*Key Reflection Questions:*
- ◆ Do students feel like they belong at school?
- ◆ Can they talk about things that matter to them?
- ◆ Do they feel cared for by adults and peers?
- ◆ Are students celebrated when they succeed?

## Competence

*Guiding Questions:*
- ◆ What practices affirm students' abilities and strengths?
- ◆ How can we help students feel capable of completing challenging tasks?
- ◆ What practices are limiting students' growth and sense of competence?

*Key Reflection Questions:*
- ◆ Do students feel capable of managing tasks on their own?
- ◆ Do they know what they are good at and how to help others?
- ◆ Are they utilizing tools like checklists and rubrics to achieve success?

## Autonomy

*Guiding Questions:*
- ◆ What practices empower students to take ownership of their learning?

- How can we help students develop their ability to make choices and express their ideas?
- What practices are preventing students from feeling independent?

*Key Reflection Questions:*
- Do students feel they can be themselves at school?
- Are they setting goals and achieving them?
- Do they have a say in how to correct mistakes and solve problems?

## Moving Forward: A Plan for Strengthening Relatedness, Competence, and Autonomy: What Students Need, and Adults Must Foster

As a result of this reflection process, the Bellflower team identified several immediate steps to begin addressing gaps in students' experiences of relatedness, competence, and autonomy. These actions are the beginning of a more significant effort to create a school environment where all students feel connected, capable, and empowered. While these strategies are meaningful first steps, the team recognizes that real change will require a long-term commitment to ongoing reflection, student feedback, and a willingness to shift power in the classroom.

### Immediate Strategies for Relatedness

To support this shift, teachers will begin scheduling one-on-one check-ins with students to gain a deeper understanding of their experiences. These conversations draw on adult SEL capacities, such as perspective-taking and emotional attunement, as well as open, judgment-free questioning. Teachers will practice staying present, noticing their reactions, and setting aside assumptions to truly hear what students share. By co-creating guiding questions with colleagues, they'll approach each conversation with humility and a commitment to relational trust.

The team acknowledges that the current academic curriculum centers on white identities and experiences. While diversifying the curriculum is not a quick fix, they will begin working with academic coaches to incorporate texts in ELA, science, and history that better reflect their students' backgrounds.

Additionally, structured collaboration opportunities will be built into classroom routines. To ensure all students contribute meaningfully, roles within group activities will be clearly defined, fostering a more equitable and interactive learning environment.

### Immediate Strategies for Competence

The Bellflower staff will temporarily pause the grading of SEL skills to reassess their approach. They recognize the need for a more holistic view of SEL that takes into account subjectivity, normativity, and bias. Similarly, the "Bounce Back Plans," which do not always reflect the realities of all students, will also be paused. However, pausing these practices is only the first step. The team will need to determine what meaningful alternatives look like.

Teachers will use reinforcing language at least twice daily to support students' sense of competence, identifying academic and social successes. Feedback will be specific and constructive, such as, *"I saw how you used the strategy we talked about to solve that problem. That shows real persistence,"* or *"You took a risk by sharing your idea. How did it feel to speak up in front of the group?"* The team recognizes that true competence-building requires more than teacher feedback; future steps will involve helping students identify and reflect on their own growth.

Additionally, homework will become optional as the team reassesses its role in student learning.

### Immediate Strategies for Autonomy

The team will introduce checklists for significant projects and assignments to help students stay organized, track their progress, and clarify the steps needed for success. While this is a helpful tool, genuine autonomy requires more than structure. It requires giving students authentic opportunities to make decisions about their learning. The team acknowledges that this area requires further development, including ways to give students a greater say in classroom practices and problem-solving approaches.

## Looking Ahead

These initial strategies respond to the reflection process, but are not the end of the work. Looking ahead, the team will assess whether these changes make a real difference in students' experiences and refine their approach accordingly. The goal is to implement new strategies and foster a school culture where students' voices have a meaningful impact on the learning environment.

## Final Thoughts

Gabriel's experience is a powerful reminder of how well-intentioned SEL practices can fail students if the realities of their lives are not considered and if adults have not done their own inner SEL work to recognize bias, remain curious, and respond with humility and care. When we focus solely on coping strategies and desired behaviors without understanding student context, we ask students to suppress their true selves and emotions, a form of gaslighting, whether intentional or not. Now that Sarah and her team understand Gabriel's reality, they can work toward creating conditions where all students can learn.

This shift aligns with Lily Zheng's definition of equity in *DEI Deconstructed*, which includes both "the presence of well-being and success across all groups" and "the absence of discrimination and mistreatment for all groups" (Zheng, 2021). While we may not be able to remove every systemic barrier students face, we can start by examining and revising the very practices that contribute to inequity. Our responsibility is to ensure that our actions promote well-being and eliminate discrimination within schools and classrooms.

As leaders, we are responsible for the policies that guide our schools and the practices that teachers implement. To lead with responsiveness and care, we must first cultivate our own social and emotional competence. This involves engaging in perspective-taking, regulating our emotions, and reflecting on how our identities influence the learning conditions we create.

In Chapter 3, we will examine how this inner work is both a personal endeavor and a foundation for shaping the external conditions that support adult SEL. Engaging in deep reflection and intentional action can foster a school culture where equity and social-emotional learning thrive, leading to meaningful growth for both students and adults.

### Bringing it Back to You

- How can you assess and reflect on your identity, biases, and experiences to better understand how they influence your leadership and interactions with students and staff?
- How can you ensure that the policies and decisions you make at the school or district level reflect a commitment to equity, especially for students from marginalized groups?
- What immediate steps can you take to create an environment promoting relatedness, competence, and autonomy for students and staff? How will you measure success in these areas?

### Bringing it Back to Your Team

- How does your team currently assess and address your students' cultural, socioeconomic, and identity-based needs in SEL practices? Where do you see gaps, and how can you address them collaboratively?

- What specific practices or structures in your school or district unintentionally reinforce deficit-based thinking about students? How can your team shift to an asset-based approach that acknowledges the strengths of all students?
- How can your team ensure that SEL programming and practices are responsive to the lived experiences of students, especially those from marginalized communities? What actions can you take to engage students in co-creating these practices?

# Part 2

## The Inner Work of SEL We Need to do The Outer Work of Equity and Justice

# 3

# Self-Awareness

> **Big Ideas in This Chapter**
>
> ♦ Self-awareness is foundational for equity leadership. It helps leaders recognize how emotions, thoughts, and identities shape their behavior, and how that behavior impacts others, especially those most often marginalized.
> ♦ The body is a source of insight. Learning to tune into physical sensations helps leaders regulate stress, stay present, and respond intentionally in moments of challenge and tension.
> ♦ Intentional Change Theory offers a roadmap for equity-aligned growth. It guides leaders through defining a vision, recognizing current patterns, learning new approaches, and experimenting with change in practice.
> ♦ Growth doesn't happen in isolation. Honest feedback and supportive relationships are essential for bridging the gap between how leaders intend to show up, and how others actually experience them.

Self-awareness is the foundation of both social and emotional learning (SEL) and equity-centered leadership. In the previous chapters, we examined how SEL must be universally embedded into Tier 1 instruction and how dominant cultural norms, particularly white normativity, can shape its implementation in ways that reinforce exclusion rather than belonging. But ensuring that SEL serves all students equitably requires more than just shifting instructional practices. It also requires classroom conditions that support growth and learning.

In this chapter, we shift our focus from students to ourselves, the adults leading SEL efforts. Grounded in Richard Boyatzis's *Intentional Change Theory* (2024), we'll explore a structured approach to cultivating self-awareness. Through case studies and practical exercises, we will examine how emotions, thoughts, and behaviors intersect, and how our values and identities shape leadership and interactions. By understanding the relationship between one's "Ideal Self" and "Real Self," we can develop meaningful strategies for personal growth and drive sustainable, equity-centered SEL initiatives within our schools and communities.

## Case Study: Georgetown Public Schools

Vanessa was recently hired as Assistant Superintendent of Support Services in Georgetown Public Schools, a large urban district in the Northeast. She oversees special education, school climate and culture (including SEL and discipline), positive youth development, and alternative education.

Georgetown serves over 20,000 students across nearly 40 schools. The student population is 48% Hispanic/Latino, 24% White, 20% Black, 6% Asian or Pacific Islander, and 2% multiracial. Roughly 70% of students qualify for free or reduced-price lunch. Discipline data reflect national disparities: Black students are suspended at three times the rate of white students; Latinx students at twice the rate. A recent district survey found that 39% of middle schoolers and 62% of high schoolers identify stress as a significant issue, often attributed, without clear evidence, to COVID-19 and social media. There is an emerging push to normalize students acknowledging their emotional needs.

Principals report that stress is disrupting learning: chronic lateness, absenteeism, and behavior concerns are up. The district has discussed shifting from punitive discipline to restorative approaches and strengthening student SEL competencies. They want students to be able to identify coping strategies and self-regulate.

To support this, Georgetown has increased mental health staffing. Each school now has at least one school adjustment counselor; all high schools also have a Dean of Students responsible for climate and culture. Middle and high schools have Climate and Culture Coaches who focus on non-classroom learning environments.

Vanessa, who previously worked in Chicago, is struck by the district's insularity—many leaders are Georgetown alumni, and long tenures are common. "People never leave," she has been told. Despite the investment in staffing, she sees little infrastructure for mindset or skill development. She's concerned about the discipline and engagement data and is launching a year-long Adult SEL professional learning series for leaders at the schools with the most concerning patterns. The goal is to deepen understanding of SEL as a foundational shift, not an add-on, so leaders can model and lead this work in their buildings. I'm a consultant on this project, coaching Vanessa and several principals.

One of them is Steve, principal of Uptown High, one of the district's more affluent schools. Steve attended Georgetown schools himself and now has three children in the district. He's skeptical of the SEL push, calling it "just the district's latest flavor of the day." While he acknowledges that students are stressed, he attributes it to a lack of resilience. "Everyone's stressed. That's life," he says. "Kids today have no sense of reality." Steve believes in consistency and tradition—"If it ain't broke, don't fix it"—and sees the school as functioning well, despite data suggesting otherwise. Though dismissive of the SEL focus, he admits that his perspective as a white man limits his understanding of some student experiences. He's uneasy about the shifts ahead but wants to remain open. Each principal brings a different version of resistance or hesitation. Vanessa senses this and worries about how sustainable her position will be. Still, she's committed to creating lasting change.

We'll return to this case later in the chapter as a lens for examining the real challenges of leading equity-centered SEL work in systems shaped by history, identity, and inertia, and considering how these insights can inform our leadership.

## A Holistic View of Self-Awareness

Many believe self-awareness is about identifying what makes us feel negatively activated or recognizing our habitual responses. While these are important first steps, at its core, self-awareness involves seeing the intricate connections between our physical sensations, emotions, and thoughts and understanding how they shape our behavior and relationships. It calls us to recognize the values, beliefs, and identities that guide our actions and to examine how these show up in different contexts, influencing how others experience us.

This level of self-awareness also asks us to reflect on moments when our values manifest in ways that may be unhelpful or even harmful. Consider a leader who deeply values "achievement." While this value might inspire high expectations, it can lead to rigid control, a reliance on strict discipline, or a preference for quick fixes. Such behaviors, though well-intentioned, can erode trust. By contrast, a leader who values collaboration may approach achievement differently, fostering open dialogue and listening to diverse perspectives. They may lean into collaboration and shared decision-making. These behaviors build trust and empower everyone to play a meaningful role in shaping the school's vision for success.

Understanding how our values shape our choices is a critical aspect of self-awareness. When we bring a compassionate curiosity to our patterns, we gain the ability to reinforce behaviors that align with our aspirations and challenge those that do not. In doing so, we create space for ourselves and others to thrive. Self-awareness, then, is a quiet yet transformative act that holds the power to shift the culture and climate of our schools from the inside out.

Self-awareness also requires us to reflect on how our actions are experienced by others and the impact they have. A principal who consistently listens, collaborates, and communicates openly helps build a culture of trust. In contrast, behaviors that come across as inflexible or dismissive can create distance and resistance. While reputation can reflect these patterns over time, it is ultimately shaped by the ways we show up and the choices we make. Understanding the connection between our behavior and its impact helps us lead more intentionally and effectively.

This connection between self-awareness and reputation underscores why self-awareness is essential for social-emotional learning and leadership. It influences our ability to build trust and navigate conflict. Yet, the gap between perception and reality is more significant than most realize. Research indicates that only about 15% of people are truly self-aware, with a correlation of less than 30% between how we perceive ourselves and how others perceive us (Eurich, 2018). This disconnect can have real consequences, as a lack of self-awareness undermines decision-making, collaboration, and relationships.

By cultivating a deeper understanding of how others perceive us, we can align our actions with our intentions, bridging the gap between who we think we are and how we present ourselves in our schools and communities. This work isn't easy, but it is transformative for ourselves, those we lead, and the culture we hope to create.

## Intentional Change Theory

We can begin the self-awareness journey by adapting Richard Boyatzis's Intentional Change Theory (ICT), a tool helpful for thinking about lasting and sustainable personal and organizational change. ICT is a four-step process that offers a roadmap for reimagining who we are and how we lead, with the ultimate aim of creating lasting change:

1 **Define your ideal self:** Imagine the kind of person and leader you want to be.
2 **Understand your real self:** Reflect on who you are today and how you show up.

3 **Learn:** Gain new skills and insights to grow and improve.
4 **Experiment:** Try new actions to practice becoming your Ideal Self.

To change the institutions we work within, we must first change ourselves. This work is not easy. Change can feel daunting, especially if we haven't envisioned what's possible on the other side. Without a clear vision, a sense of purpose, and a commitment, it's too easy to falter under resistance.

When we engage in equity-related changes, we should anticipate that there will be resistance. And resistance will come. It always does. I recall one district where a newly hired Director of Diversity, Equity, and Inclusion initiated a series of courageous conversations, engaging staff in reading, reflection, and dialogue around identity, privilege, power, and implicit bias. While many were ready to dive into this long-overdue work, other staff decried it as "reverse racism." Complaints escalated, families got involved, and tensions boiled over in public forums.

This mounting pressure exposed a deep misalignment between the superintendent and the Director of DEI. While the Director had a clear vision for advancing equity and was prepared to lead staff through the discomfort and resistance that meaningful change brings, the superintendent was unprepared for the backlash. Rather than standing in solidarity with the Director or reinforcing the district's commitment to equity, the superintendent responded by imposing a "moratorium on DEI" under the guise of "self-reflection." This decision revealed a lack of preparation, vision, and shared purpose at the leadership level, collapsing equity efforts under external pressure.

By contrast, I've seen what happens when leaders approach equity work with deep personal preparation, when they root themselves in their vision and values and build the capacity to navigate resistance with clarity and resolve. These leaders don't avoid discomfort; they anticipate it. They move forward with a careful balance of courage, empathy, persistence, and adaptability, understanding that equity work is a long game requiring sustained effort and resilience. Unlike the superintendent who wavered under pressure, these leaders act in concert with their teams, ensuring a unified approach. Resistance doesn't derail them or force retreat. It becomes a catalyst for deeper engagement, reinforcing their commitment and sustaining momentum even when external pressures mount.

At its core, ICT emphasizes the power of envisioning a better version of ourselves and committing to it. Positive visualizations, rooted in hope, joy, compassion, and optimism, act as biological catalysts, activating the parasympathetic nervous system and unlocking the creativity and openness necessary for meaningful transformation. ICT reminds us that lasting change is sustained not just by strategy or compliance but by the emotional resonance of what is possible.

Equally vital are the relationships that hold us through the process. No one deepens self-awareness in isolation. We need people who call us into our best selves: colleagues, mentors, partners, and friends who challenge us with care. These are the ones who celebrate our wins but also identify areas where we need to grow, refusing to be passive supporters when more is required. As leaders, we must not only seek this kind of support but also offer it to those we lead, ensuring that equity work is not just an individual pursuit but a shared commitment.

## ICT Step 1: Define Your Ideal Self

Richard Boyatzis designed ICT as a framework for achieving personal and organizational transformation, not explicitly as a tool for equity work. However, its principles offer a foundation for launching equity-centered leadership.

As meaningful as goals like "becoming a collaborative leader" or "aligning reputation with intentions" might be, they do not inherently advance equity unless explicitly tied to it. Without a deliberate commitment to equity-centered leadership, the systems and behaviors that perpetuate inequity will persist. By applying ICT through an equity lens, we can use this process to imagine not only who we want to be but also how our leadership can disrupt the status quo and create meaningful change for those with marginalized identities.

Leaders in many schools, including those in the case study, carry the responsibility of equity-centered leadership. This work is not optional. Yet, the pathway to enacting such leadership is deeply personal. It demands that leaders reimagine possibilities for change in ways that align with their unique values and identities.

In his book *The Noble School Leader* (2022) and through his work with Noble Story Group, Matthew Taylor offers a powerful framework for applying ICT to evoke self-awareness and guide this reimagining. Taylor's approach emphasizes operationalizing emotional intelligence (adult SEL) in a way that allows leaders to clarify their vision and lean into the challenges of school leadership.

 **Activity: Defining Your Ideal Self: Visioning Your Equity Leadership**

Inspired by Taylor's methodology on self-awareness, I've adapted a series of reflective questions to center equity specifically. As you read each question, pause, close your eyes if you are comfortable, and visualize your response. Focus intentionally on what you want to achieve. Resist the tendency to dwell on what you fear, wish to avoid, or have experienced in the past.

- Who do you want to be as an equity leader? This is where we state the desired result we envision. Do you want to be a leader who increases the diversity of your staff or creates communities where interpersonal behaviors and policies support the belonging of historically marginalized students and staff?
- What would being an equity leader look like and sound like for you? This is where we name what we would do and say to live into who we want to be. Do you want to

be a leader who is empathetic and a good listener or one who paces their work in a way that prioritizes historically marginalized students and staff?
- How would being an equity leader feel in your body? Here, we notice how our bodies would feel if we lived into equity work, including sensations, muscles, and energy. Is it more important to feel comfortable and at ease or to feel eustressed, energetic, and excited?
- What emotions would you experience as an equity leader? Here, we name the precise emotions accompanying living into our vision. Is it more important to you to feel calm, reassurance, and certainty, or challenge, determination, and resilience?
- What thoughts would accompany being an equity leader? This is where we name what would be happening for us metacognitively. Are you a leader who will be thinking, "How do I make everyone comfortable with this?" or "What biases might I be bringing into this situation?" and "Am I centering marginalized voices?"
- What impact would you be having as an equity leader? This is where our change brings about a change in staff and our organization. Are you a leader who will be evaluating the impact based on your feelings or from diversity data? Or would you evaluate the impact based on equity audits, retention data, policy reforms, and resource allocation?

As you complete this visioning exercise, take a moment to hold onto the intentions and insights you've surfaced. Remember that equity leadership will never be about perfection, which is not achievable, but about consistent progress, balancing aspiration with action, discomfort with growth, and vision with accountability.

# Envisioning the Ideal: Coaching Insights from Vanessa and Steve

Let's examine how Vanessa and Steve from the case study navigated this process as I coached them through these questions and captured their reflections. Their experiences underscore a fundamental truth: we all enter this work from different starting points, shaped by our histories. The paths we take will vary. Progress in equity work isn't linear; it's iterative. Through ICT, we embrace this evolution, allowing our visions for who we want to be as leaders to shift and deepen as we gain knowledge and build skills.

| Who do you want to be as a leader who centers equity in SEL? ||
|---|---|
| **Vanessa:**<br>♦ I want to be an equity leader who balances compassion for staff who have not been challenged to change with accountability to ensure SEL is implemented in ways that promote equity.<br>♦ I want to be trusted as an equity leader with practical expertise in policy and programming, making decisions that will result in student well-being and success.<br>♦ I want to be an equity leader who is courageous and who moves forward even in fear. | **Steve:**<br>♦ I want to be an equity leader who can see how and when inequity functions in SEL and my school.<br>♦ I want to be an equity leader trusted by my staff so they always see the work as our work together and that we are learning simultaneously.<br>♦ I want to be an equity leader who creates conditions where learning and talking about equity feels safe and routine. |
| **What would being an equity leader look like and sound like for you?** ||
| **Vanessa:**<br>♦ There's no opt-out; we are using SEL as a lever for equity.<br>♦ Adults must do the work before bringing it to the students.<br>♦ Let's assess the current reality in our schools side by side using X criteria. Here are my evidence-based observations. What do you see?<br>♦ Let's examine this SEL practice and explore how it upholds inequities.<br>♦ How do our identities inform what we see and prioritize?<br>♦ Let's figure out the next steps together. | **Steve:**<br>♦ Let's redesign our student survey so the information we receive truly informs SEL decisions. Who would like to help with this?<br>♦ Help me understand what you are seeing.<br>♦ What did I miss?<br>♦ Do we need to look at this differently?<br>♦ We aren't being asked to be perfect; we are being asked to try.<br>♦ Let's build routine discussions on equity into our leadership team agenda. |

| How would being your vision of an equity leader feel in your body? | |
|---|---|
| **Vanessa:**<br>◆ On the edge of discomfort or tension in my stomach and chest, but more like a motivated or excited discomfort.<br>◆ Warm, strong, and energetic. | **Steve:**<br>◆ At ease, with a sense of comfort and lightness. |
| **In your vision as an equity leader, what emotions would you be experiencing?** | |
| **Vanessa:**<br>◆ Confidence, assertiveness, integrity, justice, and compassion. | **Steve:**<br>◆ Confidence, curiosity, connection, and support. |
| **What thoughts would accompany being an equity leader?** | |
| **Vanessa:**<br>◆ My team has got this!<br>◆ Look at the progress we are making.<br>◆ I'm so proud of our accomplishments.<br>◆ The students look happy and confident. | **Steve:**<br>◆ I'm learning; we are learning.<br>◆ We've got each other's backs.<br>◆ That wasn't so bad. |
| **What impact would you be having as an equity leader?** | |
| **Vanessa:**<br>◆ I'm not just the face of this. I'd have a growing number of public allies in the work.<br>◆ We would have an equity-centered SEL advisory group that includes families, students, and staff.<br>◆ We'd have implemented policy revisions, including discipline reform.<br>◆ Students would feel cared for in ways that matter to them.<br>◆ Consistent expectations and clear communication would shape a shared vision. | **Steve:**<br>◆ Staff and students would engage more actively in equity-centered SEL.<br>◆ Conversations would be actionable and free of jargon.<br>◆ Families and students would contribute their perspectives regularly. |

| Vanessa | Steve |
|---|---|
| **Who do you want to be as a leader who centers equity in SEL?** ||
| **Vanessa:**<br>◆ I want to be an equity leader who balances compassion for staff who have not been challenged to change with accountability to ensure SEL is implemented in ways that promote equity.<br>◆ I want to be trusted as an equity leader with practical expertise in policy and programming, making decisions that will result in student well-being and success.<br>◆ I want to be an equity leader who is courageous and who moves forward even in fear. | **Steve:**<br>◆ I want to be an equity leader who can see how and when inequity functions in SEL and my school.<br>◆ I want to be an equity leader trusted by my staff so they always see the work as our work together and that we are learning simultaneously.<br>◆ I want to be an equity leader who creates conditions where learning and talking about equity feels safe and routine. |
| **What would being an equity leader look like and sound like for you?** ||
| **Vanessa:**<br>◆ There's no opt-out; we are using SEL as a lever for equity.<br>◆ Adults must do the work before bringing it to the students.<br>◆ Let's assess the current reality in our schools side by side using X criteria. Here are my evidence-based observations. What do you see?<br>◆ Let's examine this SEL practice and explore how it upholds inequities.<br>◆ How do our identities inform what we see and prioritize?<br>◆ Let's figure out the next steps together. | **Steve:**<br>◆ Let's redesign our student survey so the information we receive truly informs SEL decisions. Who would like to help with this?<br>◆ Help me understand what you are seeing.<br>◆ What did I miss?<br>◆ Do we need to look at this differently?<br>◆ We aren't being asked to be perfect; we are being asked to try.<br>◆ Let's build routine discussions on equity into our leadership team agenda. |
| **How would being your vision of an equity leader feel in your body?** ||
| **Vanessa:**<br>◆ On the edge of discomfort or tension in my stomach and chest, but more like a motivated or excited discomfort.<br>◆ Warm, strong, and energetic. | **Steve:**<br>◆ At ease, with a sense of comfort and lightness. |
| **In your vision as an equity leader, what emotions would you be experiencing?** ||
| **Vanessa:**<br>◆ Confidence, assertiveness, integrity, justice, and compassion. | **Steve:**<br>◆ Confidence, curiosity, connection, and support. |

| What thoughts would accompany being an equity leader? | |
|---|---|
| **Vanessa:**<br>◆ My team has got this!<br>◆ Look at the progress we are making.<br>◆ I'm so proud of our accomplishments.<br>◆ The students look happy and confident. | **Steve:**<br>◆ I'm learning; we are learning.<br>◆ We've got each other's backs.<br>◆ That wasn't so bad. |
| **What impact would you be having as an equity leader?** | |
| **Vanessa:**<br>◆ I'm not just the face of this. I'd have a growing number of public allies in the work.<br>◆ We would have an equity-centered SEL advisory group that includes families, students, and staff.<br>◆ We'd have implemented policy revisions, including discipline reform.<br>◆ Students would feel cared for in ways that matter to them.<br>◆ Consistent expectations and clear communication would shape a shared vision. | **Steve:**<br>◆ Staff and students would engage more actively in equity-centered SEL.<br>◆ Conversations would be actionable and free of jargon.<br>◆ Families and students would contribute their perspectives regularly. |
| **Vanessa:**<br>◆ I want to be an equity leader who balances compassion for staff who have not been challenged to change with accountability to ensure SEL is implemented in ways that promote equity.<br>◆ I want to be trusted as an equity leader with practical expertise in policy and programming, making decisions that will result in student well-being and success.<br>◆ I want to be an equity leader who is courageous and who moves forward even in fear. | **Steve:**<br>◆ I want to be an equity leader who can see how and when inequity functions in SEL and my school.<br>◆ I want to be an equity leader trusted by my staff so they always see the work as our work together and that we are learning simultaneously.<br>◆ I want to be an equity leader who creates conditions where learning and talking about equity feels safe and routine. |

| What would being an equity leader look like and sound like for you? ||
|---|---|
| Vanessa:<br>◆ There's no opt-out; we are using SEL as a lever for equity.<br>◆ Adults must do the work before bringing it to the students.<br>◆ Let's assess the current reality in our schools side by side using X criteria. Here are my evidence-based observations. What do you see?<br>◆ Let's examine this SEL practice and explore how it upholds inequities.<br>◆ How do our identities inform what we see and prioritize?<br>◆ Let's figure out the next steps together. | Steve:<br>◆ Let's redesign our student survey so the information we receive truly informs SEL decisions. Who would like to help with this?<br>◆ Help me understand what you are seeing.<br>◆ What did I miss?<br>◆ Do we need to look at this differently?<br>◆ We aren't being asked to be perfect; we are being asked to try.<br>◆ Let's build routine discussions on equity into our leadership team agenda. |
| How would being your vision of an equity leader feel in your body? ||
| Vanessa:<br>◆ On the edge of discomfort or tension in my stomach and chest, but more like a motivated or excited discomfort.<br>◆ Warm, strong, and energetic. | Steve:<br>◆ At ease, with a sense of comfort and lightness. |
| In your vision as an equity leader, what emotions would you be experiencing? ||
| Vanessa:<br>◆ Confidence, assertiveness, integrity, justice, and compassion. | Steve:<br>◆ Confidence, curiosity, connection, and support. |
| What thoughts would accompany being an equity leader? ||
| Vanessa:<br>◆ My team has got this!<br>◆ Look at the progress we are making.<br>◆ I'm so proud of our accomplishments.<br>◆ The students look happy and confident. | Steve:<br>◆ I'm learning; we are learning.<br>◆ We've got each other's backs.<br>◆ That wasn't so bad. |

| What impact would you be having as an equity leader? | |
|---|---|
| Vanessa:<br>◆ I'm not just the face of this. I'd have a growing number of public allies in the work.<br>◆ We would have an equity-centered SEL advisory group that includes families, students, and staff.<br>◆ We'd have implemented policy revisions, including discipline reform.<br>◆ Students would feel cared for in ways that matter to them.<br>◆ Consistent expectations and clear communication would shape a shared vision. | Steve:<br>◆ Staff and students would engage more actively in equity-centered SEL.<br>◆ Conversations would be actionable and free of jargon.<br>◆ Families and students would contribute their perspectives regularly. |

Vanessa and Steve now each have an equity vision they are working toward. These are not forever visions, but rather, they provide them with a clear target to work toward that, once accomplished, can be revised. As you can see, Vanessa and Steve are in different places in their equity leadership.

Vanessa is deeply committed to creating equity through SEL. She knows that transforming the district's approach to SEL means changing mindsets, engaging in challenging conversations, and creating a shared understanding of what equity looks like in practice. Her focus is on courage—moving forward despite fear and ensuring that equity is advanced through strong decision-making and accountability.

Steve's reflection centers around collaborative leadership. He has yet to learn how inequities function within SEL and the school setting. While open to learning, he's focused on ensuring safety and consistency rather than embracing the change Vanessa envisions.

As Vanessa and Steve each work toward their equity visions, how might their different approaches—Vanessa's focus on courageous decision-making and Steve's emphasis on building trust and safety—impact the pace and sustainability of equity-driven change in their respective schools?

Now that you've begun to articulate your Ideal Self, the next step is to explore the gap between who you hope to be and how you show up today. The journey from vision to transformation is rarely linear. In Part 2 of our self-awareness exploration, we explore how equity-centered leaders confront the messy, human realities that surface when they begin working toward their visions for themselves in real time.

## ICT Step 2: The Real Self

Why can't we instantly achieve the vision we set for ourselves? Because the journey toward growth is rarely uncomplicated. The most important part of self-awareness is understanding what stands in the way, not externally, but within ourselves. Richard Boyatzis's ICT defines the Real Self as who we are right now, encompassing our current emotions, behaviors, values, strengths, and weaknesses. The Real Self is often a tangled knot of contradictions, shaped by experiences and beliefs that quietly disrupt our progress.

The Real Self is a reflection of the stories we've internalized, the habits we've formed, and the comfort zones we cling to. Recognizing the Real Self requires deep honesty and a willingness to see the ways we might sabotage our own aspirations.

This inner work of self-awareness asks us to face what is deeply uncomfortable. Why do certain conversations about equity make us uneasy? What biases or fears are we holding onto that block us from engaging fully? What stories do we tell ourselves? Maybe that we're "good" people who don't need to change, or that failure is something to avoid at all costs? It's in these moments of messy, often humbling confrontation with our own humanity that real transformation begins to take root.

Equity centered self-awareness is an ongoing practice, a commitment to return again and again to the truths we might prefer to avoid. It requires us to sit with discomfort, to notice when our defenses rise, and to choose curiosity over judgment toward ourselves and each other. Over time, we come to understand that seeing what holds us back is not a sign of weakness, but of strength and courage.

To develop a deeper understanding of the Real Self, I often guide people to identify what prevents them from embodying their Ideal Self in the present. This exploration begins with broad observations about challenges or barriers, but the real insights come when they recount a specific moment that illustrates the issue. By reflecting on the details of that experience they uncover deeper struggles influencing their behavior.

The following table contains examples from Vanessa and Steve as they reflected on their journeys toward equity leadership. These narratives reveal how self-awareness grows from the interplay of general observations and vivid, personal moments.

| Person | General Challenges | Specific Moments |
| --- | --- | --- |
| Vanessa | I tend to move fast, too fast for others. I know the way schools operate doesn't work for many children and staff, and we don't have a lifetime to fix it. But I lose my compassion when adults prioritize their comfort over how we treat children. I work in explicitly equity-focused spaces, but I'm often told to back off because "people aren't ready." I feel like I'm always taking the heat, while those not doing the work face no consequences. | During a superintendent's cabinet meeting, a white colleague pulled me aside during a break to give unsolicited advice. She said I was "too intense, borderline aggressive," and making principals "uncomfortable." She suggested I ease up, that she was looking out for me and my ability—and she used these exact words—ability to be successful. |
| Steve | I'm a matter-of-fact person and dislike emotional currents in conversations. I can be terse when I sense people are upset or when caught between competing priorities—like explaining district initiatives to staff I don't fully understand or support. The district is very top-down, and I think that replicates in my own communication style, particularly during emotionally charged situations. | I led a staff meeting about announcements, including my schedule for SEL and equity work. The staff caught me off guard with questions I wasn't ready to answer, like: "Will we have time for SEL in our day?" and "Does this mean no more accountability for students?" |

Now you are invited to do the same work to help you explore and deepen your understanding of your Real Self. By reflecting on both general challenges and specific moments where you felt disconnected from your Ideal Self, you can uncover the patterns and behaviors that get in the way of your growth as an equity leader.

>  **Activity: Explore Your Real Self**
>
> Begin by identifying a general challenge or barrier that prevents you from fully showing up as your Ideal Self. Consider what often pulls you away—fear, conflict avoidance, perfectionism, or something else.
>
> Now, ground your reflection in a specific moment. Describe a time when you felt disconnected from your best intentions. Where were you? What were you doing? What were you hoping to achieve, and how did the situation unfold?
>
> For example:
>
> ◆ Did a meeting where you intended to advocate for an equity revision to a policy leave you silent because of tension in the room?
> ◆ Did fear of upsetting a colleague lead you to stay quiet when you noticed a microagression?
> ◆ Did frustration with feedback make you react defensively instead of with concern?
>
> Write down the details telling the story of that moment.

## ICT Step 3: Learn

The next part of ITC is Learn. I've mapped out five key areas of self-awareness, through which I guide Vanessa and Steve as they continue their journey. But before we delve deeper into their experiences, let's pause to consider the concept of neuroplasticity—the brain's remarkable capacity to adapt and change—and how it shapes not only our personal habits but also our broader systems of interaction and response. Then, we'll return to Vanessa and Steve's progress.

## Neuroplasticity and Our Habitual Responses

Self-awareness has its roots in the body, specifically through the sense of interoception. Interoception is your ability to perceive what's happening inside your body, an internal radar that detects signals from your organs and internal systems. It helps you notice basic needs, like hunger, thirst, or fatigue, and more subtle cues, like your heartbeat, breathing patterns, muscle tension, or that fluttery sensation in your stomach when you're nervous.

This bodily awareness is vital because physical sensations are often the first indicators of a chain reaction. Think of these sensations as the first domino in a sequence; they provide early warnings that you might be veering off course emotionally or behaviorally. When we cultivate interoception, we gain the ability to recognize and interrupt these patterns early, stepping into self-management before the dominoes tumble too far.

Over time, our bodies develop habitual responses to challenging, overwhelming, and even traumatic experiences. These unconscious "maps" are formed through repeated reactions to stress and are deeply embedded in both the brain and body. Resmaa Menakem (2017), in *My Grandmother's Hands*, explains that racialized trauma is not just psychological, it is stored in the body and passed intergenerationally. He describes how somatic (body-based) responses, like a racing heart, clenched jaw, or tight shoulders, are often tied to historical and collective experiences, not just individual encounters. This means that when engaging in conversations about race and equity, both white individuals and people of color may experience bodily activation, though for different reasons.

Similarly, Beverly Daniel Tatum (1997) discusses how racial identity development influences emotional and physical responses in discussions about race. White individuals, often unaccustomed to addressing privilege, may feel physiological discomfort, such as tightness in the chest, and shallow breathing, not because they are in danger, but because they are experiencing cognitive and emotional dissonance. Meanwhile, people of color may experience similar bodily sensations tied to past dismissals, racial microaggressions, or patterns of exclusion. More recent research extends this understanding, emphasizing that such interoceptive responses are not simply personal reactions but are shaped by social context, systemic inequity, and the ongoing development of racial identity (Rivas-Drake et al., 2023). This underscores why interoception is not just a personal skill, but one profoundly influenced by racialized experiences.

## Interoception and Equity Work

What's essential to understand is that we cannot reason our way out of a stress response. This is especially true in white Western cultures, where the emphasis has long been placed on the workings of the mind over the wisdom of the body. Yet, when it comes to managing somatic stress in equity work, the path to regulation lies in the body itself. Learning to notice, interpret, and regulate bodily signals is key to staying engaged rather than retreating or shutting down in moments of discomfort.

To develop greater interoception, we must practice tuning in to our internal sensations. While this takes time and patience, it's a skill that can be strengthened with consistent effort.

- Mindfulness practices, such as body scans, help cultivate an intimate awareness of internal signals.
- Self-check-ins throughout the day build interoceptive awareness. Pause to ask:
  - How is my breathing?
  - Do I feel tension in my muscles?
  - How does my stomach feel?
- Journaling bodily sensations over time helps identify patterns and improve regulation.

Equity work activates the body. Feelings of discomfort, defensiveness, or avoidance often surface in response to the vulnerability required for meaningful dialogue. By becoming an expert in recognizing your body's specific reactions—how activation feels for you—you can begin to regulate those responses rather than letting them control you.

Below is a table capturing Vanessa's and Steve's reflections on their bodily sensations as they cultivated interoception. Use this as inspiration for your practice of tuning in to your internal signals.

| Vanessa | You know that moment when your body locks up—when a wave of heat floods through you, tightening everything from your shoulders to your throat? It's like your body is sounding an alarm before your brain even catches up. That's what happened to me. My chest felt tight, my breath shallow. I could hear the room, see the faces, but I felt frozen, as if I couldn't move or respond the way I wanted to. |
| --- | --- |
| Steve | The first sign was my lip twitching—that's how I know I'm under stress before I even register the emotion. Then my hands started shaking. I gripped the microphone, but I knew if I held it too long, people would see. So I put it back in the holder, trying to steady myself, trying to push past the physical reaction so I could focus on the conversation. |

After hearing Vanessa and Steve's reflections on their bodily sensations during challenging moments, let's turn the lens inward to your own experiences.

 **Activity: Physical Self-Awareness**

Reflect on that moment when you weren't at your best—a time when stress, frustration, or discomfort got the better of you. What did you feel in your body? Were there clear signals that your body was activated? Ask yourself:

- ◆ Did you feel flushed?
- ◆ Did you have a knot in your stomach?
- ◆ Did you notice sweat or clammy palms?

> - Was your breathing shallow or rapid?
> - Did you feel tension in your shoulders, neck, or jaw?
>
> Take a moment to pause, tune into your memories, and notice the physical sensations that accompanied your emotional state. Write down what you can remember.

## Key Area Two: Emotional Self-Awareness

Physical self-awareness is deeply connected to emotional self-awareness. By tuning into the signals your body sends, like tense shoulders or shallow breathing, you can better understand how different situations and stressors manifest both physically and emotionally. This awareness creates space for more intentional responses instead of automatic reactions.

Neuroscientist Lisa Feldman Barrett, in *How Emotions Are Made*, challenges the traditional view that emotions are hardwired, universal reactions, like instinctively feeling fear at the sight of a snake or joy at a birthday party. Instead, she argues that emotions are constructed in the moment, shaped by our body's signals, past experiences, and the surrounding context. In other words, emotions are not fixed responses; they are predictions our brains make to help us respond to the world around us.

For example, if you've worked in an environment where your ideas were consistently dismissed in meetings, your brain might predict frustration or unease before your next team discussion. Similarly, if past equity conversations have left you feeling vulnerable or scrutinized, your brain may anticipate anxiety before those discussions even begin. This is where interoception, the ability to sense internal bodily signals, becomes critical. A racing heart, clenched jaw, or tight shoulders aren't just physical sensations, they are part of how your brain constructs emotional experiences.

The same bodily sensation can feel entirely different depending on the context. A racing heart might signal excitement when you're about to contribute to a conversation where you feel valued, or it might indicate anxiety if you fear saying the wrong thing during a discussion about racism. Barrett's research shows that we are not trapped by these predictions. By shifting our thoughts, reinterpreting situations, or even making small physical adjustments, we can influence how we feel and respond. For example, if your heart is racing before speaking in a tense meeting about equity, it might not just be self-doubt, it could be the weight of past exclusion or the fear of reinforcing harm. Instead of internalizing that sensation as personal inadequacy, you might reframe it as a signal of commitment, a sign that this conversation matters. Taking a slow breath and grounding yourself in your purpose can help you shift from feeling on the defensive to stepping into intentional engagement.

This insight is powerful in equity and justice work. Emotional self-awareness helps us recognize how our own experiences within institutions shape our emotions and, in turn, how those emotions influence our actions. By deepening this awareness, we build the capacity to engage in difficult conversations with greater resilience and intention, rather than being overwhelmed by past emotional patterns.

## The Ripple Effect: Emotional Contagion

Emotions don't exist in isolation. They spread, shaping the tone of our interactions and the energy of a space. When someone speaks with warmth and enthusiasm, we are likely to feel uplifted. Likewise, stress, frustration, or detachment can ripple outward, affecting everyone in the room. This phenomenon, known as emotional contagion, happens largely outside our awareness. Research shows that when we observe another person's emotions, our brains and bodies often respond in kind, unconsciously prompting us to reflect those feelings ourselves (Liu et al., 2022).

What's particularly important is that we are more likely to absorb the emotions of those we see as powerful or central to our social environment. This means that leaders, whether in classrooms, organizations, or communities, have an outsized influence on the emotional climate of their spaces (Xie, He, & Gan, 2021). A leader who remains calm and grounded can foster collaboration and creativity, while a leader who is visibly stressed or disengaged can leave their team feeling drained and disconnected. The way we show up emotionally affects those around us, shaping how equity conversations unfold and whether people feel safe, valued, or dismissed.

## Reflections in Action: Vanessa and Steve

Vanessa and Steve's experiences illustrate how emotions and physical sensations intertwine in high-stakes conversations, particularly those involving equity and justice. The table below captures their reflections on how they felt in moments when they didn't show up as they had hoped:

| Vanessa | Steve |
| --- | --- |
| Outraged, humiliated, othered, alienated, misunderstood. | Rattled, unnerved, flustered, perturbed, unprepared. |

Their experiences reflect more than just personal discomfort; they reveal how systemic inequities and power imbalances shape emotional responses. Vanessa's feelings of alienation and being othered echo the ways institutions reinforce exclusion, making it difficult for those with marginalized identities to feel fully heard and valued. Steve's sense of disempowerment and unpreparedness speaks to the anxiety many feel when navigating discussions about race, power, and privilege, particularly when they fear causing harm or exposing gaps in their understanding.

---

 **Activity: Emotional Awareness**

Recall a moment when you didn't show up as you had hoped. Think about the emotions you felt. If you have access to an emotions list, use it to be as precise as possible.

---

## Key Area Three: Metacognitive Self-Awareness

Metacognition is the ability to think about your thinking, to monitor and adjust your thought processes as needed. First explored in depth by developmental psychologist John H. Flavell in the 1970s, metacognition helps us approach challenges with greater self-awareness (Flavell, 1979). Whether you're studying for an exam or navigating a difficult conversation, metacognition enables you to reflect on what's working and what's not so you can pivot. It's a skill many educators are familiar with and often teach students to use: think about how you learn, evaluate your strategies, and adjust the ones that work best to succeed.

Metacognition is also a critical tool for understanding ourselves, especially in emotionally charged or challenging situations. When we're activated or overwhelmed, we often fall back on habitual thoughts and beliefs. Some of these patterns, known as self-limiting beliefs, can constrain our potential and prevent meaningful action. These beliefs aren't always unfounded. Many are rooted in real experiences, societal pressures, or fears, but they can often be distortions that hold us back.

For example, imagine you're in a meeting about equity and think, "I can't speak up because I'll probably offend someone." This belief may stem from a fear of unintentionally offending someone, or it may stem from fear of not being liked by colleagues because you disagree with them. While it may seem protective, when this kind of thinking keeps you silent, it stalls equity progress and places an unfair burden on those already engaging in equity-centered dialogue and action.

Or consider the thought, "I can't engage in this work if they make it feel so unsafe." Robin DiAngelo's concept of white fragility sheds light on this reaction. It refers to the defensiveness or emotional overwhelm some white individuals feel during discussions of race, often stemming from fears of being perceived as racist or as "the bad guy" (DiAngelo, 2018). Again, this response may seem like self-protection, but it shifts the focus away from the work at hand and onto the individual's discomfort, stalling progress in the process. Recognizing this as a habitual reaction allows for deeper self-awareness and intentional action.

Metacognition gives us a way to pause and ask, "Why am I thinking this way? What patterns or past experiences might be shaping this belief?" In doing so, we create space to challenge these thoughts. For instance, reframing "I'll just make things worse" into "I can approach this conversation with humility and learn if I misstep" opens the door to participation and growth. Similarly, reframing "I can't engage if it feels unsafe" into "Discomfort is normal. I can tolerate discomfort to stay focused on the work" shifts the focus back to the larger purpose of equity efforts.

White leaders, who are the least directly affected by systemic injustice, must confront and unpack their self-limiting beliefs. Metacognition plays a vital role in this process. It empowers us to push past fears of inadequacy or discomfort and engage with courage and intention. And in equity work, this matters deeply.

As you read Vanessa's and Steve's reflections, notice the equity-related self-limiting beliefs embedded in their automatic thoughts. These are patterned, internalized narratives shaped by experiences, telling them what's possible—or not.

| Vanessa | Steve |
|---|---|
| "Here we go again. I've been here before, and I can't win." | "How did I become the spokesperson for this work?" |
| "How dare she. How dare she undermine me. They're triangulating, and they're against me." | "I'm not the district. Don't blame me for their initiative. I'm one of you." |
| "I might as well quit now. Seriously, how did I not seeing this coming?" | "They're probably right. We will get punished. And everyone will hate me in the process" |

 **Activity: Metacognitive Awareness**

Take a moment to return to that event where you didn't show up the way you wanted to. What thoughts ran through your mind? Write them down without judgment. Ask yourself: How might these beliefs be impacting my ability to show up as best self? As an equity leader?

## Key Area Four: Identity Self-Awareness

Identity self-awareness is essential for school leaders striving to create school communities of belonging. It begins with exploring the elements that shape who we are, our worldview, values, and belief, which ultimately guide how we interact with those in our school community.

It's equally important to recognize the intersectional nature of our identities—the way our race, gender, class, and other social categories intersect to shape our experiences and relationships and position us in relation to power and advantage. Legal scholar Kimberlé Crenshaw (1989) first introduced the concept of intersectionality to explain how multiple social identities interact to create unique experiences of oppression or privilege. In schools, intersectionality plays a critical role in shaping how students experience belonging, discipline, and academic opportunities, often in ways that remain invisible to those in positions of power. For school leaders, this means being conscious of how their identities influence their leadership decisions, and how they shape school policies and practices.

For example, consider a school leader from an affluent background who now works in a school serving students from low-income communities. Their life experiences might lead them to lower expectations for students, assuming that poverty inherently limits academic interest and potential. The Pygmalion Effect, first demonstrated by Rosenthal and Jacobson (1968), and reaffirmed by a 2022 meta-analysis by De Boer et al. (2022), underscores how educators' expectations (shaped by our identities) can significantly influence student outcomes—often with lasting effects on achievement over time.

The reflections below reveal how Vanessa and Steve's identities influenced their experience in that moment when they felt they didn't show up as their best selves.

| Vanessa | Steve |
|---|---|
| "There's the obvious part of my identity of being a Black woman and having the repeated experience of being accused of being pushy, bold, aggressive, and being put in my place by white women. And then having self-doubt. Was I aggressive? Was she just trying to help me? I love who I am, but this part of me that I love keeps me on the edge, and it can feel dangerous. But there are other parts of my identity that are important in this work. I'm the daughter of an activist. I'm highly educated. I have my PhD. And I have practical skills and knowledge and expertise that I have gained from years of hard work. I've earned the right not to be second-guessed about my work." | "I come from a family of high achievers who have chosen more lucrative careers than I have, and I am the classic middle child. I'm constantly trying to prove myself. I have an intense fear of failure, being wrong, and not being good enough. I do not like being at odds with people. I also know I'm a white man, and the way things work here right now works well for me and my children. But not everyone in this community benefits. I'm not sure what to do with this part of my identity yet. I am also quite comfortable in the transactional but not the emotional space. So, when I sense others are reacting emotionally, I tend to shut down." |

 **Activity: Identity Self-Awareness**

Take yourself back to the moment you reflected on earlier. What aspects of your identity were at play? Consider how they influenced your response or actions. Becoming aware of these dynamics helps us grow more intentional in how we show up—for ourselves, our students, and our communities.

## Key Area Five: Reputational Self-Awareness

Our physical sensations, emotions, thoughts, and identities quietly shape our actions, often in ways we don't fully realize. These actions impact those around us, influence our organizations, and ultimately define how we are perceived over time.

Reputational self-awareness is the ability to recognize how our behaviors and decisions affect other people. It is understanding how our behavior builds or erodes trust and how our actions either reinforce or disrupt inequities in our spaces.

Yet, self-perception is not always reliable. We tend to judge ourselves by our intentions, while other people experience us through our impact. This disconnect can make it difficult to recognize when our actions contribute to harm or perpetuate inequities. Identity also plays a role. Our lived experiences shape how we interpret situations, the perspectives we prioritize, and the assumptions we carry into decision-making. Without intentional feedback, we risk moving through our roles unaware of the patterns we create.

Seeking direct, honest feedback is essential for bridging the gap between intention and impact. Anonymous 360-degree feedback can uncover trends in how our leadership is perceived, helping us move from assumption to awareness. But we don't have to wait for formal feedback to start building this awareness.

To support this process, I asked Vanessa and Steve to revisit a moment when they felt they had fallen short as equity leaders and reflect on three questions:

- What did I do in that particular situation?
- What was the impact of my actions on myself, others, and my organization?
- Has anyone confirmed or shared feedback about these impacts?

Without feedback, we are often left to guess at our impact, and sometimes, those guesses are wrong. The reflections below capture Vanessa's and Steve's insights into how their actions shaped perceptions and trust. Use them as a guide to explore your own impact.

| Vanessa | Steve |
| --- | --- |
| What did I do in this particular situation? ||
| I swallowed my rage, acted grateful for her feedback, thanked her, and didn't ask questions. I went into the bathroom and cried, and then I put on my big kid pants and returned to the meeting as if nothing had happened. | I appeared annoyed and defensive. I think I said something paternalistic: "Now is not the time to worry about something that hasn't happened yet." I shut them down and inadvertently suggested the changes may never come. |

| Vanessa | Steve |
|---|---|
| What was the impact of what I did, on myself, others, and my organization? ||
| The impact is that now I'm full of self-doubt. I'm second-guessing every word I say to principals. I'm having difficulty seeing the good in them because I'm worried they're talking about me behind my back. So, I'm not working as effectively or collaboratively as I want to. And my colleague now had my consent to undermine me further. And worst of all, I don't know what happened. | The impact is that I may have reinforced an us-them view of me and them. I certainly wasn't collaborative. I acted as if they didn't have the right to ask questions and dismissed their concerns. I've made it more challenging for myself to create conditions in which they'll view this situation as us being together. |
| Have others confirmed any of the impacts? ||
| No, not at all. I haven't talked to anyone about it. | My leadership team and I debriefed. They agreed with my assessment of how I handled the situation. |

Most of us can recall a moment when our intentions didn't match our impact. Use the activity that follows to examine your own leadership moment with the same clarity.

>  **Activity: Explore Your Reputational Self-Awareness**
>
> Go back to that moment when you didn't know up as your ideal self. Ask yourself the following three questions:
>
> ◆ What did I do in that particular situation?
> ◆ What was the impact of my actions on myself, others, and my organization?
> ◆ Has anyone confirmed or shared feedback about these impacts?

## ICT Step 4: Experiment

The experiment phase of Richard Boyatzis's Intentional Change Theory is where reflection meets action, where ideas about who we want to be start taking shape in the real world. After building awareness of the space between our Ideal Self and real self, this phase is where we test the waters, trying on new behaviors and approaches that move us closer to our vision.

We should not expect or strive for grand transformations or flawless execution but instead show up differently in small, intentional ways. The power of this phase lies in the practice. Some experiments will land beautifully, while others might feel awkward or even fail outright. That's the point. Every attempt, whether it works or not, brings new insights, helping us refine our approach and deepen our understanding of ourselves.

## Here's What This Looks Like for Vanessa and Steve

Vanessa will focus on building trust and addressing resistance by establishing routine check-ins with principals that combine open dialogue with progress updates on SEL and equity work. She believes these regular interactions will provide insights into their concerns and help track their growth in understanding and implementation. Vanessa plans to schedule biweekly one-on-one meetings where she can discuss challenges and successes, and collaboratively identify next steps to ensure sustained progress toward equity-centered SEL practices.

She also intends to test her ability to respond more assertively to feedback that undermines her leadership. For example, suppose someone critiques her approach or gives unsolicited advice. In that case, she plans to say, "I appreciate your concern, and I'd like to explore this further to ensure we're aligned on what equity-centered SEL means for the district."

Steve has proposed experimenting with building his understanding of equity-centered SEL. To start, he will dedicate 30 minutes each week to reading materials recommended by Vanessa and reflecting on how these ideas connect to his daily leadership. Steve plans to proactively gather staff concerns through a survey before initiating discussions about SEL and equity initiatives. This approach will give him time to prepare thoughtful responses and not feel so caught off guard. With his readings, and checking in with Vanessa for input, he will be better prepared to address concerns with clarity and confidence.

>  **Activity: Experiment**
>
> Based on what you've learned about your self-awareness, how will you experiment in your leadership? Reflect on your insights and choose one aspect of your leadership to test in practice that will move you closer to your ideal self.
>
> Afterward, reflect on the experience. How did it feel to try this new approach? What reactions did you notice from your team? What worked, and what would you adjust moving forward?

## Final Thoughts

Self-awareness is a throughline in the journey toward equity-centered leadership. This chapter emphasizes the importance of understanding the connections between our sensations, emotions, identities, thoughts, and reputations, and how these influence our equity-centered leadership.

By reflecting on the gap between our Ideal Selves and Real Selves, we gain insight into the ways we can grow, both as individuals and as leaders committed to equity and belonging. Change doesn't happen all at once; it's iterative and deeply personal. The process of experimenting with new behaviors, as illustrated by Vanessa and Steve, reminds us that progress often comes through small, intentional steps.

Take these reflections, tools, and frameworks as companions for your leadership journey. Commit to revisiting your self-awareness regularly, adapting as you grow, and holding space for both your own evolution and that of those you lead.

### *Bringing Self-Awareness Back to You*

- How has self-awareness influenced your ability to lead equity-centered SEL initiatives? Reflect on a specific moment when greater self-awareness shaped a leadership decision or improved an interaction with a colleague or student.
- What self-limiting beliefs have you identified in your own leadership practice? How have these beliefs hindered your progress toward equity goals, and what steps can you take to overcome them?
- In what ways do your identities, values, and life experiences shape how you approach leadership and equity work? How can you align your actions more closely with your intentions to foster belonging and equity in your school community?
- What strategies can you implement to cultivate greater self-awareness in your daily leadership practice?

### *Bringing Self-Awareness Back to Your Team*

- How does our team's collective self-awareness, or lack thereof, affect our ability to advance equity-centered SEL initiatives? What specific examples illustrate this dynamic?
- How do the diverse identities, values, and experiences within our leadership team influence our approach to equity work? How can we leverage these differences to create more inclusive and equitable school environments?
- How might we use tools like Intentional Change Theory to guide both personal and team growth? Discuss how visualizing our Ideal Team and understanding our Real Team could inform our leadership practices and support sustainable, meaningful change.

# 4

# Self-Management

> **Big Ideas in This Chapter**
>
> ◆ Self-management involves aligning your behavior with your values, particularly when emotions run high or situations become complex.
> ◆ Self-care is foundational to leadership. A balanced "body budget," supported by rest, nutrition, movement, and meaningful connection, strengthens your ability to stay present, grounded, and effective in the face of stress, resistance, and injustice.
> ◆ Emotions are not distractions from leadership—they are part of it. Using somatic (body-based) and cognitive (mind-based) strategies helps you stay steady, interpret your feelings, and respond thoughtfully, even in high-pressure situations.
> ◆ Self-management is not about compliance or control; it's about empowerment. It means staying aligned with your values when avoiding, deflecting, or remaining silent would be easier.

We are living in a time of chronic uncertainty. Injustice is everywhere, and we witness it in real time: climate crisis, political instability, and ongoing race- and gender-based oppression. The weight of it all can leave us feeling powerless. The question is: How do we resist that feeling of powerlessness? How do we stay steady in an unsteady world? How do we confront injustice in our schools, communities, and ourselves without losing our sense of commitment?

For me, it starts with paying attention. I read independent news every day, so I don't look away. I notice how my body feels, name my emotions, and question my thoughts when everything feels overwhelming. I let myself cry. I joined an organizing group so I don't feel alone or powerless. I take care of my body—I go to bed early, walk in the woods, and run. I stay close to the people I care about the most, and I let people care about me. I spend time with my dogs and cats, whose steady presence helps me find calm. These aren't fixes, but they help me stay human. They keep me from burning out or going numb. We don't need to buy expensive memberships or turn to wellness trends that may not feel accessible or culturally aligned. What we need are grounded, sustaining practices that keep us connected to our purpose and one another. If we're going to challenge injustice and push for institutional change, we need ways to stay resourced for the long haul.

In the last chapter, we defined visions as equity leaders, turned inward to build self-awareness, and paid attention to both mind and body, noticing how they respond to challenges and strains. However, awareness alone does not bring about change. Now, the focus shifts to action. In this chapter, we explore self-management, the everyday choices that keep us grounded and intentional. Together, we'll examine strategies that help us lead with clarity and care, sustain your growth, and strengthen our leadership.

## Case Study: Elmwood Middle School

Elmwood Middle School has long employed a "paycheck" system to manage behavior, where students lose points—or "dollars"— for infractions such as poor posture, failing to "track the speaker," dress code violations, off-task behavior, or incomplete homework. These minor offenses often result in detention or suspension, with disproportionate consequences for students with disabilities.

In 2017–18, a state investigation found that Elmwood suspended 29.1% of students receiving special education services, the highest rate in the state. By contrast, the district average was 5.8%, and the statewide rate was just 1.3%.

Elmwood serves a student population that is 1.5% White, 82.8% Black, 0.2% Asian, 14.9% Hispanic/Latino, and 0.2% American Indian/Alaska Native. Ninety-two percent of students qualify for free or reduced lunch. The school has been recognized for consistently outperforming the district on standardized tests, although scores have declined in recent years.

After the removal of a long-serving principal and a wave of leadership turnover, the superintendent appointed Cameron to lead the school in 2022–23. Her charge was clear—implement equitable social-emotional learning and replace exclusionary discipline practices with developmentally appropriate, student-centered approaches.

Cameron came from an elementary background, known for her steady presence, instructional instincts, and belief that every student wants to be seen and valued. She's warm but direct, the kind of leader who checks in often, notices the small things, and doesn't shy away from hard conversations. But middle school leadership has tested her. Some staff members dismissed her early, referring to her as a "baby principal," insisting that middle school demands a stricter approach. Many continue to favor punitive discipline and see her vision as idealistic.

The setbacks have been real. Suspension rates rose in her first semester as staff resisted change and defaulted to exclusion. A professional learning session on student-centered discipline ended in tension, with several teachers leaving the room. Some families began questioning whether the school had lost its structure. Cameron, a driven perfectionist, felt the pressure mount. She holds herself to a high standard, and the lack of immediate results has weighed on her. Still, she remains committed to her conviction that strong relationships, clear systems, and student ownership are crucial to a thriving school culture.

One evening, during a mid-year dance performance, Cameron sits beside Alannah, a veteran teacher and grade team leader. As they wait for the show to begin, Cameron casually asks how she's doing. Holding back tears, Alannah admits, "I'm not sure if I'll come back next year. There's no discipline anymore. Students roll their eyes, laugh at me, and some are so hostile I'm afraid in my own classroom. Today, Tasha threw her books and flipped a chair. It's chaos. No one is learning."

She adds, "I feel completely unsupported by my AP and the school's leadership. These kids are being rewarded for bad behavior—look at them, performing tonight. I love this school, but it feels like it's falling apart."

Cameron feels a wave of anger and dread. Alannah feels overwhelmed and unsupported, and yet her comments about students feel deeply racialized and Cameron is completely caught off guard. In that moment, Cameron knows: changing Elmwood's culture won't happen quickly or easily.

We'll return to Cameron's story later in the chapter to explore how self-management plays a role in her leadership.

## Self-Management and Obedience Are Not the Same

Too often, schools equate social and emotional learning with self-management, but the version of self-management they promote doesn't try to develop autonomy. Instead of helping students build the skills to understand themselves and make thoughtful choices, the goal becomes compliance: sit still, follow directions, don't talk back. Genuine self-management supports autonomy. It helps students develop the awareness and agency to navigate challenges, rather than just meeting adult expectations. In a classroom recently, I heard a teacher say to a student, "You aren't self-managing. Track the speaker. Track. Track. If you want to earn a point, keep tracking." The message was clear: the student's ability to earn a reward depended on whether they mimicked the behavior the teacher wanted. But that wasn't self-management. That was behavior management. And in schools, the two are often confused.

Behavior management is centered on control, getting students to act in ways adults decide are acceptable. Self-management is something else entirely. It comes from developing the internal capacity to act with intention, in alignment with one's values, while navigating emotions, biases, and the complexities of relationships and systems. When students truly self-manage, they might not behave in ways that make the adults in charge comfortable.

At a charter school where I was coaching, students launched a campaign to challenge a dress code they saw as oppressive and disconnected from their identities. The policy banned "unnatural" hair colors, prohibited all headwear—hoods, bonnets, hats—and required a uniform of khaki pants, black belts, black shoes, and white button-down shirts. One teacher explained it dryly: "They need to look like business casual white men."

In response, students wrote letters, gathered signatures, and spoke at board meetings. They organized, presented their case, and attempted to work within the system. When their voices were ignored, they made a different choice. The day after the board meeting, they arrived at school in direct defiance of the dress code: hoods up, bonnets on, streaks of pink and green in their hair, jeans, and sneakers. They weren't acting out. They were acting with purpose. They were self-managing, and the adults in the building didn't know how to respond. So instead of listening to students with curiosity and the intention to understand, the school doubled down on enforcement.

If we are serious about self-management, not as a tool of control but as an essential human skill, we need to rethink how we teach and practice it. That begins with the understanding that no single strategy works for every person or situation. It means recognizing that the purpose of self-management is not to make people more compliant or cooperative. It's to cultivate the ability to make choices rooted in self-awareness and a clear-eyed understanding of power.

Rules, agreements, and expectations are crucial for maintaining safe and high-functioning schools. However, when they're arbitrary or enforced without context, they become about control rather than care. Consider the rule that requires students to "track the speaker," keeping their eyes on the person speaking at all times. On the surface, it's framed as respectful. However, in practice, it overlooks the fact that students focus and process information differently. Penalizing students for not "tracking" doesn't support engagement; it enforces a narrow, adult-centered standard of compliance.

The same is true for rules that ban colorful hair, restrict certain clothing styles, or require students to sit with their hands folded. These policies don't make schools safer or more productive. They send a different message, that conformity matters more than belonging. And students see through it. They recognize when rules are more about control than about supporting their learning. Educators can, too. Many are required to follow rigid mandates, such as scripted curricula or pacing guides, which are often framed as beneficial for students but are actually about exerting control over teachers. If we can tap into our own experiences of being managed rather than trusted, we can gain a deeper understanding of how students feel. When rules are enforced without attention to context or intention, it erodes trust. We should never confuse rule-following with self-management. Self-management enables students to develop the awareness and agency they need to make intentional, values-driven choices, rather than just avoiding punishment.

## Self-Management Is About Emotions

Many of us have learned, either directly or indirectly, that strong emotions can be a problem. But often, the problem isn't the emotions themselves. It's how society responds to them. In many schools and workplaces, especially those that prioritize control over connection, strong emotions are treated as disruptions. They're dismissed, punished, or pathologized, especially when they come from women and people of color. But emotions are information. When we pay attention to them, we gain insight into ourselves and into one another. The issue isn't that emotions are disruptive; it's that institutions have problematized them.

For years, we've been told a simplistic story about the brain: a primitive "lizard brain" controls our survival instincts (fight, flight, or freeze), while the neocortex manages logic and reason. According to this myth, when emotions take over, we lose control, and only by engaging the rational brain can we regain composure. However, modern neuroscience has debunked this notion. There is no separate "lizard brain." Emotions are not confined to a single part of the brain. They are constructed through complex processes involving multiple regions. They shape every decision we make, even when we believe we're purely rational (Barrett, 2017).

In dominant U.S. culture, emotional expression is often equated with weakness or unprofessionalism, whereas self-control is viewed as a marker of professionalism and maturity. However, these norms aren't universal and are deeply influenced by race, gender, and power. Women are often dismissed as too emotional to lead. Black people, especially Black women and girls, are labeled angry or aggressive for expressing justified frustration. In schools, this plays out in how adult perceptions shape discipline. A white student who slams a locker in frustration may be perceived as having had a rough day. A Black student engaging in the same behavior is more likely to be perceived as threatening or defiant. These patterns reflect how emotions are racialized. Black and Brown students are disproportionately punished for showing emotion, while LGBTQ+ students are often seen as disruptive simply for expressing themselves in environments that don't affirm who they are (Morris, 2019). Many of us have been conditioned to believe that controlling emotions means suppressing them, that professionalism requires detachment, and that composure equates to neutrality. But suppressing emotions can lead to stress, burnout, and disconnection (Harris, 2023). Ignoring emotions doesn't make them disappear. It only makes it harder to understand ourselves and each other. If we want fair and humane schools and workplaces, we must stop treating emotions as a liability and start recognizing them as powerful tools for understanding and change.

## Emotions Are Predictions—And That Has Everything to Do With Equity

For decades, scientists have been uncovering surprising truths about how our brains function, which challenge our understanding of our experiences. We like to believe we react to the world in real time: a hand comes too close to our eyes, and we flinch; a friend sends a GIF, and we smile; we walk into a bakery, and our mouths water. It all feels automatic, like simple cause and effect. But the reality is more complex. Our brains aren't just responding to the world. They're predicting it.

Before you consciously react, your brain is already guessing what's coming next. Imagine leaving a restaurant and walking down a dimly lit street at night when you hear quick footsteps behind you. Before fully registering the sound, your brain draws on past experiences and signals a potential threat. Your body tenses, and your heart races long before you've had time to think it through. However, if those footsteps turn out to belong to the waiter returning the credit card you left behind, your brain quickly adjusts, softening your fear response and filing away the new information for future reference. This predictive process happens constantly because the world is uncertain. To help us navigate it, our brains stay one step ahead, scanning the environment and preparing us to act before we're even aware.

These same predictive processes shape not just our emotions but also our perceptions of one another. Our brains make quick judgments based on past experiences, both personal and cultural. Suppose we've been conditioned to associate academic potential with a particular race, gender, or personality type (remember normativity from Chapter One). In that case, we may overlook students who don't fit that mold, even when they demonstrate talent, skill, and motivation.

For instance, consider a classroom where, during a fast-paced discussion, a teacher consistently calls on male students for math problems, subconsciously associating mathematical aptitude with boys. These split-second decisions can marginalize female students, reinforcing gender stereotypes and undermining their confidence in the subject. In another example, a Muslim student wearing a hijab is repeatedly asked by teachers if she's feeling too warm or if she's allowed to participate in physical activities. Although these questions may be intended as caring, they are rooted in assumptions about Muslim people. Well-meaning but misinformed instincts can still cause harm, making students feel singled out, othered, or treated as exceptions rather than as part of the community.

These predictions happen in milliseconds, often outside conscious awareness, yet they shape our decisions with real consequences. Research has shown how these unconscious predictions reinforce systemic inequities. For example, one study found that teachers are more likely to use "blaming" language when describing misbehavior by Black students compared to their white peers, leading to disproportionate disciplinary actions against Black students (Owens, 2023). Another study found that math teachers who believe gender equality has been achieved tend to be biased against girls' abilities in math, leading to an underestimation of girls' capabilities and discouraging their participation in STEM fields (Copur-Gencturk, Thacker, & Cimpian, 2023). Our brains, shaped by cultural narratives and systemic patterns, predict and perceive reality in ways that uphold existing biases, even when we believe we're being fair or objective.

Because past experiences shape emotions and biases, they can also be reshaped. When we slow down and notice our emotional responses, we create space to question our automatic assumptions. We can ask: Is this reaction based on what's happening, or on something I've been conditioned to expect?

I've recognized it in myself more than once. After twelve years in Catholic school, struggling with the disconnect between stated religious beliefs and historical othering and atrocities, and with a father who often quoted Marx's line about religion being the opiate of the masses, I emerged not only as an atheist but also with a deeply conflicted relationship with religion itself. I held (and hold) a bias where, if someone began a conversation by sharing their religious beliefs, I assumed they were more interested in signaling their virtue than in demonstrating it through their actions.

When Jeff was transferring to our school, I met his family during the intake process. Often, but not always, transfers occurred because students had been moved from one school to another due to behavioral issues. Families were understandably anxious, sometimes defensive, and trying to reframe their story before it got told for them. And for me, there was always the question: Who am I getting? What happened at the last school? What's not being said? I was trying to read between the lines before I even knew the student. Jeff's parents repeatedly emphasized that they were "good, God-fearing people," and said their children were respectful and well-behaved. I nodded through the rest of the conversation, having predicted Jeff's behavior would surely be a problem.

A few days later, Jeff was walked to my office, a space students often used to read, finish assignments, or meet in small groups. His teacher said he was "distracted… and maybe a little distracting" and could use a quieter place to work for a little while. *"Of course, that didn't take long,"* I thought. But I caught myself. I didn't even know Jeff. I was reacting to something his parents had said. And underneath that, my response was shaped by years of conflicted feelings about religion.

So I stopped. I identified the reaction, reminded myself where it came from, and made a choice: to see Jeff for who he was, not as a stand-in for his parents or my past. I asked how he was doing and if he needed anything to get started. That was it, no overcorrection, no forced connection. A simple reset that allowed the relationship to begin on its own terms.

This is what equity-centered self-management looks like: noticing where our reactions come from and choosing to respond with intention rather than habit. Recognizing our own patterns is essential, but it's only the beginning. Lasting change requires that we also examine and disrupt the systems that reinforce those patterns.

Emotions and biases aren't fixed; they're learned. And what's learned can be unlearned, if we slow down, stay honest, and practice responding differently. But individual practice alone won't undo inequity. Systems shape our thinking through the way we label students, assign consequences, structure classrooms, and even manage the transfer of students from one school to another. If those systems remain unchanged, self-management, no matter how skillful, won't be enough. We must change ourselves and the conditions that shape who and what we expect in the first place.

## Categories of Self-Management

Day-to-day, equity-centered leadership also depends on concrete, practiced strategies, tools we use in real-time to manage ourselves in challenging moments and stay aligned with our values. These strategies help us pause before reacting, ensuring our responses are guided by intention rather than impulse. They enable us to make thoughtful decisions and maintain our commitment to equity, even under pressure. I think about self-management in three categories:

- **Self-Care:** This is the backbone of self-management. Taking care of ourselves through rest, nutrition, movement, and connection keeps us grounded and prevents burnout. Without it, staying regulated becomes a struggle.
- **Body-Based Strategies:** Physical practices like breathing and movement help reset the nervous system when emotions take over. These strategies return the body to a steady state so we can respond rather than react.
- **Mind-Based Strategies:** Our thoughts drive our emotions. Practices like precisely naming emotions, reframing, and mentally rehearsing help shift unhelpful patterns so we can respond with clarity and intention.

## Self-Care

The body budget, a concept introduced by neuroscientist Lisa Feldman Barrett, explains how our brain's primary function is to manage and balance the body's energy, much like a financial budget. Outside of our awareness, our brain regulates breathing, digestion, body temperature, and the nervous system, constantly allocating energy to keep us functioning. Every experience we have either makes a deposit into our body budget or takes a withdrawal from it. Physical injuries, arguments, unwanted physical contact, lack of sleep, hunger, dehydration, and trauma all deplete our reserves, making it harder for our brain to maintain healthy function. In contrast, self-care, getting enough sleep, eating well, staying hydrated, spending time with loved ones, and engaging in exercise or recreation restores our balance.

When our body budget is in good shape, we feel energized and better able to recover from setbacks. However, when it becomes depleted, we experience fatigue, stress, and difficulty thinking clearly or managing our emotions. Under these conditions, emotions can feel overwhelming. In times of high stress, self-care becomes even more critical.

Consider how this plays out in daily interactions. If I work with someone who's a jokester, I might enjoy their humor when I'm well-rested and in a good place. But if I've just dealt with multiple crises and feel emotionally and physically drained, that same humor might feel irritating, even tone-deaf. I may snap at them or ignore them, not because they've changed, but because my depleted body budget leaves me with less capacity to engage.

While self-care *should* be a basic right, the reality is that it's often a privilege shaped by access and circumstance. Picture this: two students walk through the school doors at the same time, but they're carrying vastly different loads.

One of them woke up in a quiet home, well-rested after a full night's sleep in their own bed. They had a warm, nutritious breakfast waiting for them, and when they got stuck on a homework question the night before, a parent was there to help. Their morning was calm, maybe even encouraging.

Now, picture another student. They spent the night juggling responsibilities far beyond their years, watching younger siblings while their mother worked the overnight shift. They fell asleep on the living room couch with the TV still glowing in the background, skipped dinner because there wasn't enough food to go around, and faced their homework alone. This student arrives at school tired, hungry, and already stretched thin before the day even begins.

And yet, both students are now sitting in the same classroom, facing the same expectations. They're supposed to concentrate, stay regulated, collaborate, and meet academic goals as if they started from the same place. However, here's what's often overlooked: if the second student manages to stay engaged, meet goals, and participate fully, it won't be recognized as giftedness, even though it takes extraordinary abilities to endure that level of challenge and still engage.

Being an equity-centered leader means understanding that self-management, the ability to manage stress, emotions, and behavior, is not simply a matter of willpower or discipline. It is deeply influenced by the environment a person is navigating. When we expect students or our colleagues, for that matter, to regulate themselves without acknowledging the weight they may be carrying, we set them up to fail. Worse, we risk misinterpreting their struggle as a lack of effort, rather than as a sign of unmet needs.

Our job, then, is not just to teach strategies for self-care or emotional control, but to actively create environments that make those things *possible*. That means noticing who's falling through the cracks, advocating for systems that provide real support, and building spaces where people feel seen, safe, and valued. Because when the starting line isn't the same for everyone, equity is helping each member of our school community get what they need to thrive.

## Cameron's Self-Care

The most visible versions of self-care in popular culture often center on activities such as yoga, boutique fitness classes, massages, or wellness retreats, which can be expensive, time-consuming, and often take place in spaces that don't feel welcoming or accessible to everyone. For some, stepping into a yoga studio or a wellness space can feel more like entering a performative, privileged bubble than a place of restoration. And for many educators, especially those who are already stretched thin, the pressure to "find time for self-care" can feel like just another unrealistic expectation. Instead of replenishing, it adds guilt or stress.

That's what Cameron realized. Under the weight of her new leadership role, self-care had quietly slipped away. She took stacks of work home, ate dinner at her laptop, skipped her workouts, and often woke up at night with her mind racing. So when Alannah made a charged comment about students being "aggressive" and "hostile," Cameron froze. And while freezing is an entirely human response, her depleted physical state made it even harder to recover in the moment, and for many moments that followed.

Cameron knew that wasn't how she wanted to show up. She wanted to reengage with Alannah, not just to challenge the harmful narrative that blamed and adultified students, but also to challenge Alannah to grow. To do that well, she needed to be able to think clearly, stay grounded, and remain steady in what might be a challenging and winding conversation. That kind of leadership required strategy and stamina.

So Cameron began with a reset. She established boundaries around her work, leaving at a consistent time and limiting the amount of work she took home. She scheduled weekly dinners with friends to reconnect and rediscover joy. She restarted her morning runs, not for fitness goals, but because the movement helped release stress. And she created a wind-down routine in the evenings, turning off screens early, reading something unrelated to work, and giving herself time to unwind.

These small but deliberate acts helped her rebuild her "body budget"—that is, her emotional and physical reserves. Slowly, Cameron felt more like herself again. And with that restoration came more energy to lead the way she wanted, with presence, purpose, and genuine care.

Take a moment to reflect on your routines. What do they make possible, or less possible, for how you show up? And how might your version of self-care look different from the ones we're told to aspire to?

> **Activity: Self-Care Reflection**
>
> What comes up as you read about Cameron and the importance of self-care in self-management? Are there self-care routines you have been neglecting? How can you ensure you are energized and well-prepared to have equity-centered conversations?
>
> Take a few minutes to reflect on your current self-care practices:
>
> 1. Identify one self-care habit you've maintained and one you've neglected recently.
> 2. Consider how these habits affect your ability to manage stress and engage in challenging conversations.
> 3. Write down one small, actionable step you can take this week to strengthen your self-care routine.

## Body-Based Strategies

Sometimes, no matter how much we try to talk ourselves out of an emotional reaction, our body doesn't get the message. A friend of mine, who grew up in a home where yelling was constant and threatening, once had a panic response during a tense staff meeting, just from the sound of a raised voice. They knew intellectually they weren't in danger, but their body reacted as if they were. That's the thing about stress: it doesn't just live in the mind, it lives in the body.

This is where somatic practices come in. Strategies such as deep breathing, grounding exercises, or simply noticing physical tension can help interrupt a stress response before it takes hold. These practices activate the parasympathetic nervous system, allowing the body to return to a state of calm. Stress shows up in tight jaws, clenched stomachs, and shallow breathing. Learning to recognize those signs early allows us to respond with more choice.

But we need to name the context. Somatic tools can be helpful, but they don't fix the conditions that cause harm. When the source of stress is racism, economic precarity, or persistent exclusion, the problem isn't internal; it's structural. Using breathing techniques to manage a microaggression doesn't undo the harm of the system that allows it.

We also have to be honest about how mindfulness practices often show up in schools and workplaces. Many have been co-opted from their cultural origins and repackaged through a white, often elitist lens. This repackaging can alienate people who might otherwise benefit from these practices, or worse, it can pathologize their responses to real injustice, suggesting the problem lies within them rather than in the systems they're reacting to.

At the same time, not all stress stems from structural harm, but it still lives in the body. Cameron from our case study knows this well. She often feels a tightness in her core and a wave of nausea that comes and goes with the day's stresses. When Alannah spoke to her, it felt like she couldn't breathe; her sympathetic nervous system flooded her with adrenaline. It's a common physical response: stress neurons are heavily concentrated in the heart, lungs, and gut, which is why intense emotions can make us feel literally sick.

To support Cameron, we explored somatic practices that she could integrate into her school day in ways that felt authentic and doable, no yoga mat or meditation cushion required. The goal wasn't to push a prescribed idea of "calm," but to help her stay in her body and feel resourced.

For some, somatic grounding may involve tuning into the breath or performing a body scan. For other people, it might be dancing to a favorite song between meetings, doodling during planning time, or stepping outside for five minutes of sunlight and fresh air. These are all somatic strategies; they engage the body to reset the nervous system. What matters is the sense of relief and re-centering that is *felt*.

Cameron began again by using what worked for *her*. She started placing a hand on her belly during difficult meetings, which helped her slow her breath and stay connected. She practiced grounding not through formal exercises, but by feeling her feet solidly on the floor or gripping the sides of her chair, which served as tangible reminders that she was safe and present. She even reconnected with music, allowing herself to sing in her office between meetings and classroom visits. These weren't dramatic shifts. But they were hers, and they worked.

There isn't a prescribed method for somatic practices. There is a range of embodied strategies that you can choose from and tailor to fit your individual needs. The more consistently you practice, whether through stretching, humming, breathing, walking, or simply pausing to feel, you give yourself access to space, even in high-stakes moments.

Take a moment now to consider: What helps *you* reset when your body feels activated? And what somatic strategies could you reclaim or reimagine for yourself?

---

 **Activity: Rewiring Stress Responses Through Somatic Awareness**

This activity helps you tune into your body's stress signals and explore somatic strategies that feel genuine and restorative for *you*, rather than just what's popularized as "mindfulness."

### Step 1: Notice Your Stress Signals
Think of a recent moment when you felt overwhelmed. Where did it land in your body—tight shoulders, racing heart, clenched jaw? Jot down a few physical signs. The goal is to notice, not judge.

### Step 2: Try a Somatic Practice That Fits You
Select one strategy that feels achievable and genuine. Try it for 5 minutes.

- ◆ **Grounding**: Feel your feet on the floor or your back against a chair.

- **Self-Soothing Touch**: Place a hand on your chest, belly, or neck.
- **Movement**: Shake out your hands, stretch, sway to music, or dance.
- **Sensory Anchors**: Hold a warm mug, pet your dog, touch a textured object, or step outside and notice air or light.
- **Creative Expression**: Doodle, sing, knit, tap a rhythm—anything that lets your body lead.
- **Breath or Voice**: Take slow exhales, hum, or whisper something grounding.

These are all ways of regulating through the body. Pick what works for *you*.

### Step 3: Use It in the Moment
Next time stress hits, pause and use your practice—during a tough conversation, at your desk, in the car. A few seconds can shift your response.

### Step 4: Reflect
Afterward, check in. Did your body feel any different? What helped? What didn't? Keep experimenting. Over time, consistent practice builds greater capacity to respond, rather than react.

## Mind-Based Strategies

Mind-based strategies for self-management are tools we use to recognize and shift unhelpful thought patterns. These strategies help us pause, reflect, and respond in ways that align with our values, rather than reacting on autopilot.

Have you ever found yourself caught in a loop, replaying the same thought over and over? In our case study, Cameron described feeling stuck on a thought about Alannah that sounded like, "I can't believe she had the audacity to..." We've all been there. That kind of mental spiral is common, especially when our values feel violated.

As equity-centered leaders, we *will* be activated. When we know what's at stake for students if the adults in their school resist equity efforts, it's normal to feel upset, or even enraged. It would be strange *not* to react. However, if we're to be effective, we must find ways to get ourselves unstuck so that we can continue to move equity efforts forward.

This can feel especially hard in today's climate. The rise in anti-DEI sentiment makes it even more painful to lead equity efforts. For leaders of color, the emotional toll is often compounded; they may feel the sting of racism firsthand and then the additional burden of having to manage resistance to anti-racism efforts, often in ways those of us who are white can approach more intellectually or at a safer emotional distance.

Consider a school where staff equity professional development sparks backlash. A teacher interrupts to say, "We should focus on real teaching, not all this identity stuff." That moment can be intensely activating, especially for colleagues whose identities are being dismissed in real time. For a leader, this isn't just a test of what to *say*; it's a test of how to *stay*. Staying grounded in the face of such resistance requires the full range of self-management skills, including regulating emotions, maintaining physical presence, and choosing a response that reflects your values and goals. Mind-based strategies are part of that process, helping us notice what we're thinking, disrupt reactive loops, and lead with intention rather than anger or retreat.

Let's explore a few: emotional granularity, interrogating our thoughts, positive reframing, and mantras. Each of these helps us recognize what we're feeling, understand the underlying emotions, and choose a response that supports both our well-being and our leadership.

### Emotional Granularity

**Emotional granularity** is the ability to describe your feelings with precision. Instead of defaulting to broad terms like "*overwhelmed*" or "*upset*," breaking emotions down into more specific ones helps the brain sort through what's happening and often opens up a path forward.

But let's be clear: this doesn't minimize what's at stake. For many leaders, especially those of color, the emotions they experience through challenging inequities may not be just personal reactions; they could be responses to real harm. And while emotional granularity can support self-management, it doesn't erase the weight of the moment or the legitimacy of the emotions, such as anger, grief, or exhaustion, that people may feel. Naming those emotions with accuracy doesn't diminish them; it helps make them more manageable.

Take Cameron, for example. After a tense exchange with Alannah, she told me she felt "angry" and "completely overwhelmed." However, when emotions feel that intense, it can be challenging to move forward. I invited her to try using an emotional granularity wheel, just one of many available, to see if she could become more specific about what she was carrying. Here's what she identified:

- **Indignant**: "Alannah trashed students, and what she said was racist."
- **Impatient**: "This feels impossible—changing mindsets and behavior will take too long."
- **Embarrassed**: "I'm sure parents overheard us."

Once she named those feelings, she took a breath and said, "That helped. Now I'm thinking about what I might do. I need to deal with my impatience, but I also need to talk to her directly, about what she said *and* where she said it."

Getting more precise didn't erase her anger; it gave her a foothold. It helped her shift from being emotionally flooded to identifying a few next steps, even if they were difficult. Research suggests that people who build this skill are less likely to lash out, shut down, or rely on unhealthy coping mechanisms (Barrett, 2021). Even young children can develop this skill, building their emotional literacy early on.

Try it for yourself: What's one moment recently when you felt overwhelmed? What more specific emotions might have been underneath that? Naming them won't solve the problem, but it might give you just enough space to move with intention.

>  **Activity: Get Granular**
>
> When confronting biased or harmful remarks, emotions can feel overwhelming. Practicing *emotional granularity*—precisely naming your emotions can help you respond more thoughtfully and effectively.
>
> **Step 1: Name the General Emotion**
> Think of a time you heard a biased remark or prepared for an equity-focused conversation. Write down one or two emotions you felt, like *angry* or *anxious*.
>
> **Step 2: Get Specific**
> Use an emotional granularity tool (like a feelings wheel) to identify two or three more precise emotions beneath the surface.
>
> *Example:*
> *Angry* might become *indignant* (offended by injustice) or *irritated* (annoyed at repeated behavior).
> *Anxious* might become *overwhelmed* (feeling out of control) or *embarrassed* (worried about other people's perceptions).
>
> **Step 3: Reflect on Action**
> How do these specific emotions shift your understanding of the situation? What do they reveal about what you need to address? How might this change your approach?

## Interrogating Our Thoughts

Cameron found herself ruminating on the thought, "I'm in over my head." Many of us loop through beliefs that keep us paralyzed. Michele Nevarez, in *Beyond Emotional Intelligence*

(2022), reminds us, "You don't have to believe everything you think." That's a useful reminder, especially in emotionally charged situations. That being said, it is essential to recognize that some thoughts accurately reflect harm. Sometimes, when we see racism or bias, that's precisely what it is. Alannah's comments about Tasha were rooted in racist ideas. No reframing required. But not all stuck thoughts reflect truth. Some are self-limiting beliefs, internal narratives shaped by fear, past experiences, or learned helplessness. Thoughts like "I can't say anything," "They'll never change," or "This always happens" can shape how we present ourselves.

One I still wrestle with is: *They're going to think I'm difficult.* Early in my career, I was called a rabble-rouser and described as prickly. I was told I needed to learn humility, not because I was unkind, but because I intentionally challenged inequity in spaces where the norm was silence. Much later, after I named the obvious, blatant discrimination by a director against a colleague, I was told I had caused the director so much stress that she ended up in the emergency room.

But that belief didn't start there. I grew up hearing the same labels applied to my father, a community organizer, and was often told I was "just like him." The message was clear: if you speak up, you're the problem.

And the truth is, I may still be perceived as difficult. However, that label reflects someone else's discomfort with being challenged, rather than something flawed in me. I'm hired as a coach and consultant to help people face what's hard and make change. Clients seek me out because I tell the truth. The idea that I'm "too much" isn't grounded in the present; it's an old story. And like most self-limiting beliefs, if we don't acknowledge it, it will continue to influence our choices from the background. Studies have shown that cognitive reappraisal, which involves actively questioning the accuracy of these beliefs, can reduce emotional distress and avoidance behaviors (Ford & Troy, 2019). In equity work, that's essential. Fear-based silence lets harm go unchecked.

That's why I use these two questions, adapted from Byron Katie's *The Work*, to interrupt spirals of doubt:

### Is the thought factual?

Cameron's thought, *"I'm in over my head,"* felt true in the moment. But it was not a fact. When she slowed down, she remembered: she's faced hard things before. She accepted this role knowing it would be challenging, and she was confident in her ability to lead change. What she was feeling wasn't proof of incapacity. It was fear.

### If it's not factual, what else could be true?

This second question is about moving toward intentional action. Cameron asked herself what else could be true; she listed all the possibilities:

- I'm a perfectionist and get stuck when I think I'll mess things up.
- I need to talk it through with someone first.
- I don't want to be the only one holding people accountable.
- I'm uncomfortable with conflict, especially when it feels racially charged.
- I've handled harder things than this.
- I knew what I was signing up for—this is the job.

These reflections helped her regain her ability to respond. She moved from fear to intention. This kind of pause doesn't weaken our response. It strengthens it. It helps us hold staff and colleagues accountable. It prevents us from shrinking when what's needed is grounded moral courage.

Cameron still had to speak up. But by naming the fear and seeing through it, she did so with steadiness, without minimizing the harm or dodging the hard conversation. In this next activity, you can try this too.

 **Activity: Practicing Thought Interrogation for Clarity, Not Excuse**

This is a tool for slowing down when we're emotionally activated. It should not be used to minimize harmful behavior. Sometimes our thoughts reflect real harm. If, after reflection, you land on "Yes—this person was racist," or "This behavior caused real damage," trust that. This tool is to help you respond to self-limiting beliefs rooted in avoidance.

### Step 1: Identify the Thought.
Write down the specific thought that's been on loop in your mind. Be precise.

(Examples: "They don't respect me." "There's no point in saying anything." "This always happens to me.")

### Step 2: Ask, Is this Factual?
This isn't about denying what happened. It's asking whether your interpretation is the full story, or if fear, past experiences, or internalized doubt are also in the mix. If the thought *is* factual, if someone caused harm, was racist, or abused power, name it.

### Step 3: Ask, What Else Could Be True?
This question is about expanding your perspective, not softening the harm. Write at least three things that *might also* be true. These can include:

- I'm afraid of being labeled as difficult.
- I've been silenced before, and I don't want to go through that again.
- This person may be unaware, or they may hold deeply racist beliefs that have gone unchallenged.

All of that can be true at the same time. Don't use this question to avoid naming bias, use it to help you act with intention.

### Step 4: What Response Aligns with Your Values?
Given everything you've just named, what's one action that reflects your integrity and your commitment to equity? Maybe it's setting a boundary. Perhaps it's confronting someone, asking a question, writing it down, or seeking support.

## Positive Reframing

Positive reframing is the practice of reinterpreting a challenging situation in a more positive light. It doesn't mean ignoring harm or pretending everything is fine. It means recognizing the full weight of a moment and still choosing to focus on growth, capacity, or next steps. In equity work, reframing helps us stay engaged instead of shutting down, moving us out of helplessness and into agency.

Research indicates that individuals who employ cognitive reframing experience lower stress, enhanced emotional regulation, and improved interpersonal effectiveness, particularly in high-pressure, identity-relevant situations (Troy & Ford, 2020). I introduced this approach to Cameron after a difficult interaction left her spinning.

### Example

> **Initial Thought:** *This feels impossible. Changing mindsets and behavior will take too long.*
> **Spot the Language:** Words like *impossible* and *too long* reinforce hopelessness and isolation.
> **Reframe with Clarity:** *This is hard, and that's expected. Changing mindsets takes time, trust, and coaching. I know how to do all three.*
> **Notice the Shift:** Cameron exhaled. "I can breathe," she said. "This is hard work, but I'm good at building trust and coaching. I can do this."

The shift didn't come from pretending the situation wasn't hard. It came from acknowledging the truth *and* choosing a frame that opened space for movement. Reframing isn't sugarcoating. It's reclaiming your power to respond.

>  **Activity: Practice Positive Reframing**
>
> 1 **Write It Down:** Think of a recent situation that activated or frustrated you. Write the first thought that came to mind.
> *Example: I'll never get through to them.*
> 2 **Spot the Language:** Identify words that reinforce negativity, absolutes, or hopelessness.
> *Example: "Never" implies guaranteed failure.*
> 3 **Reframe with Possibility:** Add context, your own skills, or what's still possible.
> *Example: It's hard to reach them right now, but with time and the right approach, I may be able to build trust.*
> 4 **Notice the Impact:** How does this new frame land in your body? Do you feel more grounded, less tense, or more hopeful?

## Mantras

Mantras are intentional statements or affirmations that help anchor the mind in trying moments and align actions with values and purpose. They can be a powerful emotional regulation method, acting as a reset button in moments of intense emotion. Mantras should be personalized to ensure authenticity and relevance, allowing them to remind us of what matters most and help us stay grounded in our purpose.

Cameron chooses the mantra "Now or later?" She is committed to addressing inappropriate, biased, or racist remarks, no matter who they come from, but she does not want to freeze again. By remembering "Now or later?" she will either decide to respond in the moment or say, "Let's have a conversation about this, but now isn't the time or place. I'll send you a calendar invite so we can return to this as soon as possible." Both responses are action-oriented, but they also provide space to choose the right setting for the conversation and, if needed, gather thoughts and practice self-management strategies to show up at our best. Cameron wishes she had this mantra the night she sat next to Alannah; she can now see how she would have used the "later" response in that moment.

Mantras allow us to pause without retreating, to stay present, intentional, and aligned with what matters. Now it's your turn to craft one that helps you lead clearly when the moment gets hard.

 **Activity: Create Your Grounding Mantra**

Mantras are short, intentional phrases that help you stay grounded and aligned with your values in challenging moments. They guide your response, offering clarity and control when emotions run high.

### Step 1: Identify a Trigger
Consider a recent situation in which you felt stuck or reactive, like hearing a biased remark or navigating a tense conversation.

### Step 2: Clarify Your Values and Needs
What do you value in these moments (e.g., courage, patience, accountability)? What do you need to stay grounded (e.g., time to reflect, a reminder to act)?

### Step 3: Create Your Mantra
Craft a simple, memorable phrase that reflects your values and supports intentional action.

*Examples:*

- "*Now or later?*" (Decide whether to address an issue immediately or at a better time.)
- "*Pause, then proceed.*" (Take a breath before responding.)

> ◆ *"Lead with curiosity."* (Approach with questions, not assumptions.)
>
> Use your mantra to guide you when faced with challenging interactions.

## Final Thoughts

Even the most well-researched self-management strategies only work if we practice them outside the moment. Without preparation, we can't expect to access them when needed. Mental rehearsal, visualizing challenging scenarios, and practicing responses help build the muscle memory required to respond with clarity and control. Athletes, dancers, and public speakers rely on this approach because performing under pressure requires more than understanding or skill. The word *"rehearse"* originates from the Old French *"rehercier,"* meaning "to go over again" or "to repeat," underscoring that actual readiness is rooted in deliberate practice.

Cameron, for example, knows she will face resistance from staff, so she prepares by rehearsing her response in advance. She mentally walks through her routine: feeling the ground beneath her feet, wiggling her toes in her shoes, placing a hand over her belly, and hearing her mantra, "Now or later." If she chooses to do so later, she will examine her thoughts before the conversation, reframe any unhelpful narratives, and rehearse how she wants to present herself in the meeting. By repeatedly practicing this sequence in her mind, she increases the likelihood of remaining steady and intentional when the real moment comes.

> ### Bringing it Back to You
>
> ◆ When you feel triggered or disoriented by inequity, what helps you stay present rather than reactive?

- What thought patterns or self-limiting beliefs get in your way when you're leading for justice? How do you interrupt them?
- What practices—body-based or mindset-based—help you return to clarity when the stakes are high? What happens when you skip them?
- Where are you performing steadiness, and where are you practicing it? What would it take to close that gap?

### Bringing it Back to Your Team

- How do we model self-management in high-stress moments? How does our response to tension shape the emotional tone of the group?
- When bias or harm emerges, how do we create space for accountability without prioritizing comfort?
- What agreements or structures help us pause, reflect, or recalibrate during urgency or conflict? Where are those missing or underused?
- What does it look like for our team to share responsibility for emotional steadiness, especially when conversations get uncomfortable?

# 5

# Social Awareness

- ◆ Social awareness requires both reflection and action. It begins with noticing your own assumptions and discomfort, and grows through intentional choices that affirm and include others, especially those whose identities and experiences differ from your own.
- ◆ Context matters. Every interaction is shaped by historical, cultural, and systemic factors. Leaders must understand how these forces affect belonging, behavior, and perception in order to show up with empathy and clarity.
- ◆ Technical decisions carry relational weight. Policies and procedures don't exist in a vacuum, they impact people in very human ways. Equity leaders anticipate how decisions will land and engage others to co-create solutions that build trust.
- ◆ We impact each other's bodies. Our presence, language, and leadership shape how safe or unsafe people feel. Social awareness means creating environments that reduce harm and support the well-being of those most often marginalized.

How well do you understand the emotions, perspectives, and experiences of those around you? Up to this point, we have focused on examining ourselves, developing self-awareness, and practicing self-management. In this chapter, we shift our attention beyond the self, exploring what it truly means to see, hear, and understand one another. Social awareness allows us to empathize, recognize power dynamics, question whose voices are centered or silenced, and stay curious even when we feel uncomfortable.

We'll examine how biases shape perception, how systemic inequities influence experience, and how seemingly neutral policies, such as a dress code rule, carry deeper implications about belonging and exclusion. This chapter will prompt us to sharpen our awareness, challenge assumptions, and make more intentional choices in being present for those around us.

## Case Study: Lovelette High School

Lisette joined Lovelette this year as the new Dean of Culture. She is a 30-year-old former Physics teacher with a reputation for building strong relationships with students and families. She's often seen in the hallways, high-fiving students and chatting with parents during drop-off. Many staff members admire her positive energy and knack for connecting with students. However, some teachers have begun to express concerns about the inconsistencies in how Lisette handles certain school-wide expectations.

One recurring issue is enforcing the school's dress code, particularly the rule requiring students to keep the hoods of their sweatshirts down during school hours. Benny, the principal, has observed that while most teachers consistently uphold this policy, Lisette frequently allows students to wear hoodies with hoods up. While Benny values Lisette's relational approach, he's concerned about the impact of her choices. Teachers have shared with him that it's harder to enforce the dress code in their classrooms when students know they can wear hoods up elsewhere without consequence. For some staff, this has led to tension, with students arguing, "But Ms. Lisette lets us keep our hoodies up." Persistent dress code infractions have led to classroom removals and suspensions. The district has recently discouraged such practices, but they are in the muscle memory of how Uptown does school.

The school leadership team recently met with staff to review the dress code expectations. They emphasized the importance of consistency in creating a distraction-free learning environment. After the meeting, Benny hoped Lisette would try to align with the expectations. Yet, over the following weeks, he noticed little change. Students continued to wear hoods up in the spaces Lisette managed.

Benny is now at a crossroads. He deeply values the relationships Lisette has built and recognizes her positive impact on students and families. At the same time, he's grappling with addressing the need for consistency across the school. For Benny, this isn't just about hoodies. It's about upholding a standard.

This case study serves as a starting point for examining how leaders can balance the relational and technical aspects of decision-making, fostering alignment that prioritizes equity. We'll return to this scenario later in the chapter to explore how deepening social awareness can help navigate such complexities with clarity and care.

## The Green Line

One of the concepts I've found most valuable for understanding social awareness is The National Equity Project's 7-Circle Model, an innovation on the "6-Circle Model," created by Margaret Wheatley and Tim Dalmau in 1983.

The 7-Circle Model helps us understand the relationship between our work's technical and relational aspects and the broader systemic context in which they exist. At the heart of the model is a green line (gray, in this version) running through the circle's center, separating our work's technical and relational domains.

## Above the Green Line: Technical Work

The three circles above the green line represent the technical aspects of our work:

- ◆ Structure: Organizational frameworks like policies and hierarchies.

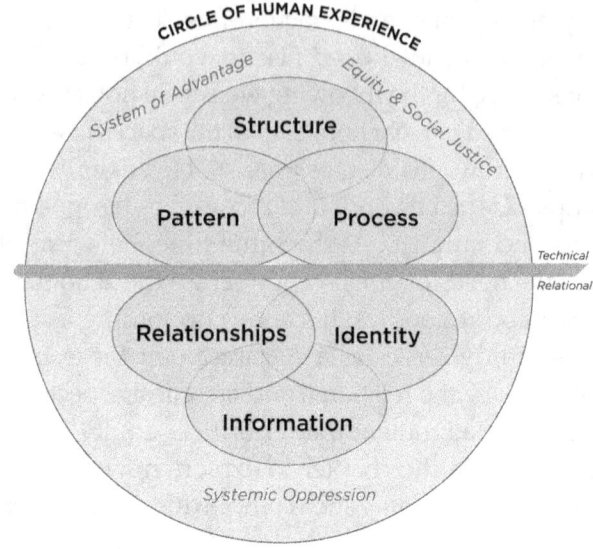

**FIGURE 5.1** The National Equity Project's 7-Circle Model

- Pattern: Repeated routines or workflows.
- Process: Mechanisms like communication protocols.

These are the day-to-day technical decisions educators and leaders make, like supervising staff, creating budgets, designing schedules, and managing discipline systems. Most coursework, professional training, and development focus heavily on these technical areas.

## Below the Green Line: Relational Work

The three circles below the green line represent the relational aspects of our work:

- Relationships: The quality and depth of connections between people.
- Identity: How personal and collective identities (culture, heritage, values, and beliefs) shape our interactions.

- Information: How perspectives and knowledge are shared and understood.

Every technical decision made above the green line inevitably impacts the relational aspects below it, influencing individuals and communities in deeply human ways. A school district has decided to implement a new literacy curriculum, selected by a central office committee with minimal input from teachers. On paper, it's a technical decision aimed at improving reading outcomes through aligned instruction and resources.

But the ripple effects below the green line are immediate and human. Teachers feel sidelined in a process that affects their day-to-day work. Some question whether the curriculum reflects the needs and identities of their students. Others feel pressure to abandon strategies they know work. As anxiety and resistance grow, collaboration breaks down, and a culture of compliance replaces one of shared ownership.

Even the most well-intentioned technical decisions shape relational dynamics. If we don't tend to both, we risk undermining the very change we're trying to create. Yet, relational work often receives far less attention in leadership training and development.

Both the technical and relational domains exist within a larger systemic context, represented by the outer circle of the 7-Circle Model: power and oppression. District A and District B, both in the same state, adopt a new literacy curriculum aimed at boosting early reading achievement. Technically, the rollout looks identical: both districts receive the same training, pacing guides, and assessment tools. Relationally, leaders in both districts work to support teachers through coaching and collaborative planning time.

However, District A is located in a wealthier suburb, where property taxes provide ample local funding. Teachers there have small class sizes, full-time literacy coaches, and dedicated prep periods. The curriculum is implemented with care, and students benefit from a well-resourced learning environment.

District B, meanwhile, serves a lower-income community with a much smaller tax base. Although they received the same curriculum, teachers face overcrowded classrooms, minimal coaching support, and outdated technology. They are expected to deliver the same results with far fewer resources.

A policy that appears neutral becomes inequitable in practice because of how historical funding structures, rooted in property taxes and residential segregation, shape what's possible in each district. Without addressing that systemic context, even strong technical and relational efforts will fall short of equity.

## Beyond the Quick Fix: Leading Through Adaptive Challenges

Understanding the difference between technical and relational, or what we often refer to as adaptive challenges, is crucial. Technical challenges are straightforward: they're the ones we can solve with existing tools and expertise. Consider creating fire drill protocols as an example; it requires coordination, but there is a clear process to follow, and the solution is rooted in logistics. Adaptive challenges, however, are a different story. They require us to reflect on our values, question our assumptions, and engage with discomfort. These challenges aren't solved with quick fixes. They demand collective learning, honest conversations, and the courage to change ourselves and our systems.

For example, many schools and districts have goals for increasing teacher diversity and treat this as if it is a technical endeavor, solvable through improved recruitment pipelines or marketing strategies. But retaining a skilled staff, particularly a diverse one, requires something more than offering competitive salaries or better schedules; those are technical solutions. The deeper, adaptive work begins when we ask why some educators feel undervalued, why staff of color are more likely to leave, or why burnout persists even in well-funded schools. Recent studies indicate that Black teachers experience significantly higher rates of burnout and are more likely to leave their positions compared to their white counterparts, often due to factors like racial isolation, lack of support, and systemic inequities within the educational environment (Center for Black Educator Development, 2023). These findings compel us to examine long-standing cultural norms, whose voices are centered in decision-making, what behaviors get rewarded, and how power is distributed in our buildings. Doing this kind of work means sitting with discomfort, listening without defensiveness, and being willing to shift our own practices, not just tweak the system around us.

We can miss the mark entirely when we treat adaptive challenges as if they were technical ones—a distinction first articulated by Heifetz and Linsky and recently expanded by Brown (2023), who applies it to the work of educational transformation. Early in my school leadership, staff mentioned they'd love a longer winter break. It seemed like a great idea. More time to rest and recharge, right? So I made a quick, seemingly straightforward decision: I extended the break to two weeks by consolidating three stand-alone holidays into it. Technically, it was efficient; it solved the immediate logistical issue and appeared to be a win.

But I hadn't considered the deeper implications. Those stand-alone days weren't just random days off—they held cultural, religious, and personal significance for many staff members. One person used a specific holiday for family traditions tied to their faith. Another counted on a long weekend in the spring for a cherished annual trip. By folding those days into winter break without consultation, I sent a message: your values don't matter here.

What I had treated as a calendar adjustment was, in fact, an adaptive challenge about how we honor the diversity of our school community and make decisions that reflect collective values. The fallout was immediate. Staff expressed frustration and disappointment, not just about the decision itself, but also about the lack of input in making it. That moment taught me that what appears to be a simple technical fix on the surface can conceal hidden complexity, especially when identity, culture, and belonging are involved.

If we don't pause to engage with the human side of our decisions, we risk damaging relationships and reinforcing inequities instead of dismantling them. Adaptive challenges require us to step back, get curious, and make space for everyone's voice. That's where the real change happens. And that takes courage.

>  **Activity: Build Trust by Considering Relationships in Every Decision**
>
> Even technical decisions—such as setting schedules, lesson plan expectations, or PTO policies—can have significant relational consequences. Before making a change, ask: Who will this affect? As appropriate, get input through surveys, team discussions, or one-on-one conversations. For example, if you're introducing breakfast in the classroom, talk with teachers first. Ask how it might affect their routines and what support they would need. When people feel heard and included, trust grows—and so does your team's willingness to engage in change.

## Lisette and Benny and the Green Line

Let's revisit the case study with Lisette and Benny. What does Benny know about Lisette above the green line?

- ◆ She often high-fives students in the hallways and chats with parents during drop-off.
- ◆ She isn't consistently upholding the dress code expectations.
- ◆ She hasn't changed her behavior following team meetings.

But what does Benny know about Lisette below the green line?

Nothing yet. He hasn't asked her any questions to understand her values or perspective. This is a critical gap in social awareness. Without engaging with Lisette, Benny is left to make assumptions—and let's be honest, assumptions are often where we get it wrong.

I often tell people I coach that when we cling to our assumptions, we miss opportunities for real connection and growth. Instead, we need to approach situations with humility and openness, as the Zen parable of "The Scholar and the Zen Master" teaches.

*In the story, a scholar visits a Zen master, eager to learn but already full of his own knowledge. As they talk, the master pours tea into the scholar's cup. He keeps pouring until the tea overflows, spilling everywhere. The scholar shouts, "Stop! The cup is full!" The master replies, "Exactly. You cannot learn if your cup is already full. First, you must empty it."*

Benny needs to "empty his cup" and consider multiple possibilities for why Lisette might be behaving the way she is. Here are several that he names:

◆ She values autonomy and prefers to make her own decisions.
◆ She wants students to like her and worries they won't if she enforces the dress code.
◆ She's not detail-oriented, so the dress code isn't top of mind.
◆ She doesn't see how her actions affect the rest of the staff.

And here's where Benny needs to refill his cup with new learning: Benny's lack of context, the cultural, historical, and systemic factors present in this situation, limit his social awareness. Policies like dress codes, especially those targeting items like hoodies or hats, often reflect deeper racial and cultural dynamics. It's not that these clothing items carry inherent cultural or racial significance; the issue lies in how meaning is imposed upon them. In many schools, educators may interpret a Black student wearing a hoodie as defiant or disrespectful, while the same item on a white student might go unnoticed or even be considered stylish. This disparity in perception leads to disproportionate discipline for students of color and reinforces harmful stereotypes about behavior and respectability (GAO, 2022).

Dress codes also often enforce narrow, binary gender norms. Girls are frequently policed for wearing clothing deemed "distracting," reinforcing heteronormative assumptions that place the burden for boys' focus on girls' bodies. Transgender and gender nonconforming students may be penalized for simply wearing attire that aligns with their identity. These students report some of the highest rates of dress code-related discipline that hinder their learning and well-being (GLSEN, 2021).

Beyond their disproportionate impact, these dress code rules are arbitrary and unrelated to student learning, undermining both student trust and instructional time. These aren't just dress code issues; they're adaptive challenges tied to identity, power, and belonging. What if Lisette's behavior is a response to these inequities? When Benny and I discuss this, he adds another possibility to his list:

She believes the policy is inequitable and doesn't want to perpetuate harm.

Again, he doesn't know for sure because he hasn't asked Lisette. But this possibility brings new insights and questions. Benny begins to understand that he can't resolve this issue by enforcing rules or asserting authority. There may be strong ethical values at play here, and he has to do some work to better understand the human and systemic dimensions of the issue.

It also raises a deeper truth about schools: sometimes the most advanced equity leadership doesn't come from those in formal positions of power. Benny holds the title, but Lisette may be further along in recognizing how institutional practices create harm. If he's willing to listen, he may not only resolve a conflict but also grow as a leader.

To move forward, Benny decides to approach Lisette with curiosity instead of judgment, preparing to learn her perspective. Here's his strategy:

- ◆ Open the conversation with a learner's mindset.
- ◆ Take time to pause and reflect if he doesn't know how to respond in the moment.
- ◆ Frame the discussion as an opportunity to collaborate and explore solutions together.

By doing this, Benny isn't just addressing a dress code issue—he's attempting to build trust and step into the kind of leadership that creates real change.

## The Conversation Transcript: Benny and Lisette

**Benny:** I wanted to talk to you about something that's been on my mind. I've noticed students breaking the dress code daily—specifically by wearing their hoodies up—and it's happening right in front of you. After our recent meeting about dress code expectations, I was surprised that it's still continuing.

You're a talented dean. You've done an amazing job building strong connections with students, and the staff really values you. This isn't a "gotcha" moment— I just want all of us on the same page. Can you tell me what's going on for you?

**Lisette:** I appreciate that framing and your asking. It's not like I mean to ignore what you said. This is hard to say, but I'll be honest: I get that the dress code has been part of the school culture here and has worked well in the past. But now, some students feel like the message is that their identities are negative or distracting—that they need to look alike to learn and be professional.

I enforced the dress code a few times, but I felt shame—literal shame—for doing it. So then I stopped.

**Benny:** I'm not sure I understand what the shame is about—can you tell me more?

**Lisette:** The dress code has become a reason for staff and students to be at odds with each other. Even the term "enforce the dress code" feels combative, like we're the militia or this is a war zone. That framing doesn't align with our values or our commitment to student and adult SEL, or equity.

Honestly, I don't understand why hoodies are such a big issue for some staff. There's no research saying hoodies interfere with learning. Yet, hoodies seem to provoke this intense reaction, like they're a personal affront to staff. Staff are usually so caring, but when it comes to hoodies, it's like all of that disappears instantly, and students feel disrespected.

|  |  |
|---|---|
|  | When I enforce something that feels demeaning to students and out of alignment with how I think adults should treat them, I feel shame for being part of it. |
| **Benny:** | Shame? That's a heavy word. |
| **Lisette:** | It's a heavy feeling. I want to feel proud of my work with students and when I feel forced to demean students, it does not make me feel proud. |
| **Benny:** | Lisette, you're giving me a lot to process. I really appreciate you being straight with me about this. I know that takes some courage. I honestly don't think anyone would know that's your perspective. I'm curious about what you would want to happen next? |
| **Lisette:** | This community cares so much about student voice and choice—you've modeled that for us, and it is the language people use here. Can we create space to hear student voices on this issue, too? For example, why do they have a voice in what project topics to do but not in what to wear? And I know staff would say we're preparing them for the real world, but they don't actually know all of the kids' real worlds. |
| **Benny:** | I'm learning, Lisette. I'm learning in this conversation. I need to sit with what you've shared because I know it has value, but it also challenges what I believe—and what we've done here—about how students should show up at school. |
|  | The uniform policy is about appearance, sure, but it's also not just about appearance. When you don't enforce the dress code, the impact is that students may think our policies are optional, and it can feel to other staff like you're undermining them. It sends a message that we don't say what we mean or mean what we say, and that makes everyone's job harder. |
|  | So I want to figure out all the parts of this. |
|  | I'm not someone who refuses to change, so when I say I'll reflect on this, I mean it. Can we reconnect next week after I've had some time to think it through? |
| **Lisette:** | Yes, of course. I appreciate that. |

## Navigating Technical Directives and Relational Impacts

The best leaders don't just check boxes or enforce rules; they inspire and motivate staff. They take the time to consider both the technical and relational aspects of every decision. And let's be clear: the purpose is not to make everyone happy. The goal is to guide people through complex challenges in a way that fosters learning and collaboration, ultimately leading to meaningful change. Balancing technical decisions with relational impacts requires leaders to know their staff as individuals and to recognize how decisions may be perceived, not just in theory but in practice. The most effective leaders don't see these as separate; they navigate both with care, knowing they are always intertwined.

And sometimes, the person modeling that kind of leadership isn't the one with the title. In this case, Lisette is the one raising critical questions about equity and impact. She's the equity leader in the room—and Benny's growth as a leader depends, in part, on his willingness to recognize that and learn from it.

Benny has emphasized the importance of consistency during staff meetings, but he and his team have never really discussed the values behind the policy. Why does it exist? What message does it send? And how might it impact different members of the school community? It wasn't until his conversation with Lisette that Benny even started to think about the relational implications of the hoodie policy.

For Lisette, the cultural and relational dynamics of the policy and the message it sends to students, particularly those with marginalized identities, matters more than the directive itself. Because these issues were never discussed openly, frustration began to build among the staff. Benny didn't see this coming, and that's precisely why social awareness is critical. This example illustrates the importance of engaging in transparent, two-way communication. True social awareness means we are always attending to the ever-present equity issues.

That means looking deeper into the context—the cultural, historical, and systemic factors shaping Lisette's perspective and the students' experiences impacted by the dress code. If we, as school leaders, don't take the time to understand how something like a hoodie policy can carry racial and cultural weight, then our social awareness—and ultimately, our leadership—is incomplete. And while hoodies may not be a flashpoint in every school, similar tensions often show up elsewhere. Perhaps in your school, the challenge lies in how homework is assigned and graded, which holidays are acknowledged, or how classroom participation is measured.

Consider how many public schools celebrate Christmas. Classrooms are decorated with Christmas trees and images of Santa; holiday concerts feature carols rooted in Christian traditions. All of this is framed as festive and harmless. But for Jewish, Muslim, Buddhist, Hindu, and atheist students and staff, the message is clear: this space centers Christian norms. They may feel pressure to participate in celebrations that don't reflect their beliefs, or to stay silent to avoid being labeled "difficult" or "not festive." What seems like a neutral celebration to some can feel like erasure or exclusion to others.

By bringing these layers into focus, Benny can learn to recognize which norms are centered and why—understanding that leadership isn't just about enforcing policy but about making decisions that reflect and respect the full humanity of the people those policies impact.

Cultivating social awareness requires understanding the systemic forces that shape the world around us. Research indicates that inequities, such as racial disparities in school discipline, are often driven by implicit biases that influence how we, as adults, perceive and interpret behavior (Tanase & Gorski, 2022). These biases do more than cause immediate harm; they can ripple outward, shaping students' experiences in profound ways. Perhaps what begins as a dress code infraction, such as wearing a hoodie, can escalate into repeated disciplinary actions, strained relationships with educators, and a growing sense of alienation from the school. Over time, these patterns, reinforced by the choices and reactions of adults, can contribute to disengagement, higher dropout rates, and even involvement with the criminal justice system. This is why doing our inner work is so important.

If we fail to examine the beliefs and assumptions that drive our responses, we risk becoming agents of the very inequities we aim to disrupt. Addressing these inequities means learning about the historical and structural forces that shape experience. Empathy is at the heart of this work. We must strive to make an emotional connection that says, "I see you, and I'm willing to do the work to make this better." That is the kind of empathy that doesn't happen by accident. It takes intentional effort to engage with different perspectives and listen to learn. We need these skills to dismantle inequities and create schools where every student feels valued and supported. To cultivate this kind of intentional empathy, we must acknowledge that many challenges in schools are not merely about rules or systems, but also about people and their relationships. The next activity invites you to practice holding both perspectives at once so you can respond in equitable and effective ways.

 **Activity: Balancing Systems and Relationships**

Think of a real challenge you're currently facing in your school or organization. It might involve a student, colleague, or policy. The goal is to examine both the technical and relational aspects of that challenge—because most issues involve both.

On one side of a page, list the systems, rules, or processes at play (the technical side). On the other side, name the ways trust or relationships are being impacted or shaped (the relational side). Are there assumptions being made? Tensions surfacing?

Once you've mapped both sides, reflect on how you might respond in a way that honors both the structure and the people involved. What adjustments could you make that address the procedural need while also building or preserving trust?

For example, if you're enforcing a new policy and it's creating tension, how might you uphold the policy while also

> listening to concerns, seeking feedback, or communicating more clearly? This process helps shift reactive decisions into more responsive, equity-centered ones.

## The Neuroscience of Social Awareness and its Role in Equity

As social beings, we constantly affect one another emotionally, cognitively, and even physically. As we explored in Chapter 4 on Self-Management, neuroscientist Lisa Feldman Barrett introduces the concept of "body budgets" to explain how our brains manage the energy needed to stay balanced and functional. This understanding is central to caring for ourselves and essential when it comes to caring for others in diverse, complex school communities.

When a brain encounters something unfamiliar, whether it's a cultural norm we haven't experienced before, a communication style that challenges our expectations, or behavior shaped by different lived experiences, it works harder to interpret it. That extra processing can show up as discomfort, fatigue, or resistance. Barrett calls this a metabolic cost: it takes more energy to connect across differences, especially when societal systems have long reinforced narrow ideas about who or what is "normal."

Importantly, "unfamiliar" doesn't just mean someone we haven't met. It can refer to someone whose identity, experience, or way of navigating the world differs from what we've been taught to expect or value. This applies to interactions across various dimensions, including race, class, language, ability, gender expression, and more. Everyone is navigating a landscape shaped by systems of power and dominant norms, so when we work to connect across those lines, there may be strain.

For those of us who belong to dominant cultural groups, we may feel a sense of resistance within ourselves. We're often not used to being out of sync with norms because those norms were built with us in mind. So when discomfort or fatigue sets in, it can feel like a signal to stop. But it isn't. It's a signal to stretch. It's far less metabolically costly to stay in our bubbles, surrounded by people, media, and messages that reflect our own beliefs, habits, and identities back to us. That's part of what makes cross-difference work feel so demanding at times. But staying in comfort zones isn't how we learn and grow, and it reinforces the very inequities we're trying to undo.

Once we begin to build our muscles, we have to be careful not to turn around and expect the same level of exposure or vulnerability from those who are already asked to do this all the time. That's why this does not mean we should force students into integration. As Beverly Daniel Tatum has pointed out, simply placing young people in shared spaces, such as a racially mixed lunchroom, doesn't automatically create connections. Without intentional structures that support authentic inclusion, students may seek out peers who share their racial, cultural, or other aspects of identity, not out of exclusion, but as a way to access safety, affirmation, and ease in environments that often feel otherwise taxing. Cultivating genuine connections across differences requires more than just proximity. It demands that adults lead by example, building our awareness, disrupting exclusionary practices, and designing spaces where all students can engage without needing to armor themselves against harm. Only then can genuine, trusting relationships grow.

Take Mr. Burns, an 8th-grade teacher who values participation and uses cold-calling to ensure students are engaged. One of his students, Alex, is neurodivergent and finds speaking up in class particularly overwhelming due to an attention disorder and social anxiety. Alex avoids eye contact, looks away when spoken to, and processes questions more slowly than her peers. When Mr. Burns suddenly calls on Alex to solve a problem, her startled response is a quiet, "I don't know." Following his "no opt-out" policy, Mr. Burns pushes her to try again. When Alex remains silent, he moves on with a sigh, saying, "You've got to be ready next time, Alex."

For Alex, this moment is more than uncomfortable. It's exhausting. Her brain works overtime to manage inputs and respond in situations that feel unsafe, and in environments that don't account for her needs. Mr. Burns, who lacks understanding of her context and, as a result, social awareness, has created a classroom dynamic that drains Alex's energy and diminishes her sense of belonging.

And Alex isn't the only one. Many students, those with learning differences, social anxiety, trauma histories, or simply quieter dispositions, can feel similarly taxed by classroom environments that prioritize rapid verbal participation. Even students who are introverted or who process more internally may experience cold-calling as a source of anxiety rather than engagement. These students often expend significant emotional and cognitive energy just trying to manage the moment, making learning more difficult and connections harder to sustain.

Now imagine if Mr. Burns had taken the time to understand Alex's context, her distractibility, her processing delays, and the anxiety she experiences when put on the spot. With that awareness, he might have reimagined participation altogether. Instead of relying solely on cold-calling, he could have offered multiple ways to engage: submitting written responses, participating in smaller group discussions, or preparing answers ahead of time with questions shared in advance. These kinds of adjustments not only support Alex but can benefit a wide range of learners.

These shifts might feel unfamiliar or require extra effort for Mr. Burns, but they would reduce barriers and create a more inclusive, responsive classroom. That's what equity-focused teaching looks like: recognizing the diverse needs students bring into the room and intentionally designing our practices to support them.

The next activity invites you to step back and reflect on how your decisions and reactions might be experienced by others, especially those whose identities and needs may differ from your own.

 **Activity: Step Onto the Balcony**

This activity helps you slow down, shift perspective, and make more informed, equity-centered decisions.

1  **Pick a recent situation.**
   Think of a decision you made or a moment of conflict with a student or colleague.

2  **Step back.**
   Imagine viewing the situation from above—like you're watching it unfold from a balcony. What patterns do you notice? Who was impacted? How might trust, relationships, or identity have been affected?
3  **Name possible causes.**
   Ask: What might be driving the other person's behavior? Could cultural background, past experiences, or school dynamics be playing a role? Write down 2–3 possible explanations.
4  **Check for unintended impact.**
   Consider: Did this decision or moment create stress or harm, especially for someone with a marginalized identity? Was anything misunderstood or overlooked?
5  **Re-engage.**
   When you're ready, return to the conversation with openness. Ask a question like:
   - "Can you help me understand what's going on?"
   - "What would support look like right now?"

   This process builds empathy and helps ensure your actions align with your values.

## The Physical Impact of Our Behavior

Our brains continuously interpret interactions, and when we perceive words or actions as dismissive, critical, or hostile, our bodies respond accordingly. Stress hormones are released, heart rates increase, and the body's regulatory systems are taxed. This dynamic is especially crucial in schools, where leaders set the emotional tone for their teams. Acting as "emotional thermostats," their words and actions ripple throughout the organization, influencing staff and students alike (Goleman, Boyatzis, & McKee, 2013).

Every interaction in schools has the potential to either relieve or intensify the stress that students and staff carry, especially those from historically marginalized groups who are navigating environments not built with their identities in mind. This impact isn't just theoretical. Research on "weathering" shows that the chronic stress of racism—being constantly on alert, experiencing microaggressions, and managing the psychological toll of exclusion—leads to worse health outcomes for Black Americans, including higher rates of hypertension, diabetes, and other chronic illnesses (Geronimus, 2023). These aren't distant, abstract outcomes; they begin in everyday environments, such as our schools.

In school settings, chronic racial stress often shows up in subtle but compounding ways. Black and Brown students may be disciplined more harshly than their white peers for the same behaviors. A student's home language might be labeled as a deficit. LGBTQ+ identities might be erased from curricula or punished through policies like dress codes or prom rules. Girls may be labeled "bossy" for the same assertiveness praised in boys. And students with intersecting marginalized identities often carry the weight of multiple, overlapping forms of stress, racism layered with classism, ableism, or heterosexism. These patterns, left unchecked, accumulate and reinforce harm.

That's why we can't confuse kindness with equity. Many educators deeply care about their students. But care alone does not dismantle racist discipline practices, biased instructional materials, or exclusionary norms. Reducing stress for marginalized students requires us to do more than simply affirm their identities; we must also change the structures and practices that harm them. That includes examining our language, policies, curricular choices, and the assumptions we make about whose voices and experiences matter.

## Final Thoughts

At its core, social awareness is the groundwork for managing relationships effectively. How we see and understand one another informs how well we can connect. Whether navigating technical decisions or engaging in challenging conversations, our ability to recognize the emotional and institutional impacts of our actions defines our capacity to lead with care and equity. Our efforts in this work can transform policies and the lives of the people and communities we serve.

### Bringing Social Awareness Back to You

- What practices can I adopt to listen deeply and understand the experiences of students, staff, and families in our community?
- What steps can I take to recognize and respond to the power dynamics within my school or district?
- What approaches do I use to understand how systemic inequities shape the experiences of others in my school community?
- How can I demonstrate empathy and humility in my interactions with others?
- What strategies am I using to foster an environment where marginalized voices are heard and valued?

### Bringing Social Awareness Back to Your Team

- What systems or policies in our school may unintentionally perpetuate inequities, and how can we collaboratively address them?
- How can we ensure that our technical decisions (e.g., policies, procedures) are informed by the relational impacts they may have on individuals and communities?
- How can we better incorporate student, staff, and family voices in our decision-making processes?
- How do we support each other in developing and practicing social awareness, particularly during conflict or misalignment?
- What professional development or resources do we need to deepen our understanding of systemic inequities and their impact on our school community?

# 6

# Relationship Management

> **Big Ideas in This Chapter**
>
> ♦ Relationship management is equity leadership in action. It's how leaders build trust, surface tension, and stay connected—especially in the face of difficulty.
> ♦ Self-awareness shapes how we lead through relationships. Inner work helps us manage defensiveness and stay grounded. Outer work is how we communicate, repair trust, and influence change.
> ♦ Discomfort is not a detour; it's part of the process. Conflict can create forward momentum when engaged with care and clarity.
> ♦ Tone-policing and calls for positivity often derail equity efforts. Leadership means naming what's hard without softening the truth to make it more comfortable.
> ♦ Power dynamics require strategic navigation. Managing up, down, and across calls for adaptability, boundary-setting, and clarity of purpose.
> ♦ Not every relationship needs to be managed. Strategic disengagement allows leaders to conserve energy and build momentum where change is possible; investing in allies builds real momentum.

How well do you build trust, navigate conflict, and foster meaningful connections in your school or district? Up to this point, we've explored self-awareness, self-management, and social awareness. Now we turn to relationship management, the space where all those skills are tested in real-time. In equity-focused leadership, relationship management carries a unique weight.

Of course, relationship management still encompasses collaborating well and getting along with colleagues. However, when we focus on equity, it becomes much more about navigating power, addressing harm, managing discomfort, and staying engaged in difficult conversations without letting changes to policies and practices that uphold inequity stall. It means knowing when to push, when to pause, and when a relationship needs to shift or end in order to remain faithful to one's values and commitments. It requires clarity, boundaries, and the courage to confront what other leaders may avoid.

In this chapter, we'll focus on what it takes to lead for equity by strengthening relationships. We'll explore how to build trust without simply placating others, how to surface and navigate tension, and how to stay connected even when conversations about equity are uncomfortable. Pursuing educational justice requires building relationships strong enough to withstand discomfort. When we practice specific skills, such as listening with curiosity, managing our defensiveness, expressing our needs clearly, and staying grounded during conflict, we strengthen relationships in ways that drive real change, rather than merely smoothing over hard truths. Our goal is to create conditions where discomfort leads to growth, and our relationships are strong enough to sustain that process.

## Case Study: Aurora Regional School District

Aurora Regional School District is a 1400-student district that serves K–12 students from multiple regions in the state. Over the past six years, the student population has undergone a steady shift, transitioning from a predominantly white, English-speaking student body to one that is now majority students of color, including 55% who are multilingual learners. Enrollment has also been declining steadily. While these changes were occurring, the school's curriculum and practices remained unchanged, with limited adaptation or support for multilingual learners. The teaching staff expressed concerns to leaders about the changing student population and requested additional support to effectively meet the needs of all students, both academically and behaviorally. To address these concerns, the school created the position of Director of Climate and Culture and hired Patricia for the role two years ago.

Patricia is deeply committed to advancing equity by ensuring that students, families, and staff experience school as a place of dignity and opportunity. Her urgency in addressing institutional inequities sometimes puts her at odds with colleagues who prefer slower, incremental change. Still, she is widely respected for her expertise and ability to drive results. She understands that creating more just and inclusive schools demands both strategic planning and persistent action. Over the past two years, Patricia has:

- Strengthened social and emotional supports for students by identifying existing services, addressing gaps, and improving access for those with the highest needs.
- Built partnerships with local agencies and brought in external experts to support staff learning.
- Helped schools design more effective, care-centered responses to student behavior, moving beyond a focus on punishment.
- Expanded support for multilingual learners and their families through translation, targeted outreach, and culturally responsive, scaffolded services.
- Launched district-wide equity and anti-racism initiatives, guiding staff to examine policies and practices that create barriers and to engage in more honest conversations about race, power, and opportunity.

Patricia has shared with me how she has experienced the quiet, insidious ways resistance to equity work shows up, through deflection, tone policing, and the ever-present suggestion that she soften her message to protect other people's comfort.

And now, events have taken an unexpected turn. Patricia had been drafting an anti-racism policy for the district's updated HR handbook, which carefully names values, aligns expectations, and sets a tone of shared responsibility. She has shared it with the leadership team for initial input twice. She has shared with them that she planned to seek early feedback from a small group of stakeholders, including high school students and families, before circulating it more widely for input, and there was consensus that the approach was a good one. However, the HR director somehow misunderstood her process and shared the draft with all staff members.

The fallout was immediate. While some staff appreciated the clarity and called it long overdue, the loudest voices were angry and defensive, saying the language was accusatory, too political, or made them feel like they were being called racist. The leadership team, caught off guard, began leaning toward damage control and appeasement, suggesting that they soften the language, delay the rollout entirely, and even consider that the staff would need time to heal from this event.

Patricia had spent the weekend fielding emails and sidelong comments, some thoughtful, others not. On Monday, the leadership team was rattled. She felt the shift in the room: the priority was definitely damage control.

At a Monday morning check-in, Superintendent Leo took a measured tone. "You've done a lot of strong work," he began. "It's amazing what you've accomplished in two years. I'm in awe of your tirelessness. But things have felt fast for the staff. This might be a good moment to slow down. Relationships are key to this work. Take the time to build them. And remember—you'll catch more flies with honey than with vinegar."

Patricia sat quietly for a beat, weighing her words. "I'm confused," she said carefully. "Mollie made the mistake. Everyone on the leadership team knew I was planning a slow rollout, gathering feedback from students, families, and making it a co-created effort among staff. It was never supposed to be shared schoolwide yet."

Leo didn't flinch. "Patricia, let me be clear, it's not just the policy. Staff have been saying for a while now that you need to slow down."

"To who?" she asked.

"To me," he said.

"To you? I've been here two years, and you've never told me to slow down. I don't understand where this is coming from."

"This was just my wake-up call. I should have said something sooner, but I'm saying it now. You're doing important work, Patricia. But it would serve you to show more patience."

His words echoed many conversations she'd had before: Make the work feel more positive. Soften the edges. Avoid making people uncomfortable. Be strategic.

And once again, she was left at a crossroads. Push forward and risk alienation, or slow down and risk compromising everything she stood for.

Patricia knew his words were not actually about relationships but about whose comfort was centered and whose discomfort was ignored. It was about the false promise of positivity, the idea that equity work could be done without tension, discomfort, or resistance. She knew this wasn't true. If it were, it would have been done already.

Later, as she told me about the experience, she described how she walked to her car following the meeting, climbed in, dropped her head on the steering wheel, and sobbed. "I permitted myself to feel all of my feelings. And then, when those few minutes passed, I wiped away my tears and reminded myself of why I'm here: for the students and staff who deserve schools built on dignity and opportunity. I'm not here to make inequity easier for staff to tolerate. I'm here to help dismantle it."

Still, she wasn't sure what her next step should be. She needed a clear strategy, not just for what to say but also for how to move within a system that often demanded her silence while expecting her labor. That meant planning in multiple directions: how to manage, where to build alliances, when to speak up, and when to walk away.

We'll return to this scenario throughout the chapter.

## The Politics of Palatability

Patricia's experience is a case study in the politics of palatability, the expectation that equity leaders must soften their edges, repackage their urgency, and make their demands more comfortable for those in power. The feedback she received carried an unmistakable subtext: be less disruptive, be more likable, and make your demands easier to swallow. This is the tightrope equity leaders walk daily.

However, this expectation is not evenly applied. Women and people of color, especially Black women, often face disproportionate pressure to align with dominant norms of communication and leadership. Their calls for justice are frequently tone-policed and dismissed as too angry, emotional, or forceful. Women who assert themselves may be labeled "difficult" or "unlikable," while Black professionals are more likely to be perceived as "aggressive" or "intimidating" when advocating for change (Livingston, 2020). These biases hinder individuals as they navigate overlapping racial and gendered expectations in systems not designed with them in mind and reinforce institutional resistance to transformation. For such leaders, the harm is compounded: first by the racism itself, and then again by the backlash that comes from naming it.

Relationship management in these moments helps us discern when and how to push while protecting our energy and career. Patricia understood that pacing for privilege, the expectation that change must unfold at a rate that does not cause discomfort to those in power, is a persistent and insidious barrier (Gorski, 2019). And while navigating that dynamic is exhausting, disheartening, and unfair, the alternative, delaying justice indefinitely, is unacceptable. So, how do leaders strike a balance between persistence and strategy, ensuring their message is heard without compromising its urgency? It requires a deep understanding of power dynamics, a willingness to disrupt strategically, and the ability to bypass traditional gatekeepers when necessary. An inherent challenge is ensuring that, in making themselves more palatable, equity leaders don't lose the urgency or conviction behind their message, or allow its seriousness to be softened for the sake of staff comfort.

This next activity invites you to reflect on your own experience walking that line, where you've felt the pull to be more palatable, and what that has meant for your leadership.

 **Activity: Mapping Your Palatability Tightrope**

Think of a time when you felt pressure to soften your message or adjust your approach to make your advocacy more acceptable. Use the questions below to reflect on what happened and how you might respond differently next time.

1 **Describe the Situation**
   What issue were you speaking up about?
   Who was in the room?
   What power dynamics were at play?
2 **Identify the Pressure Points**
   How were you expected to change your message, tone, or delivery?
   Was this pressure direct or unspoken?
3 **Analyze the Impact**
   What happened after you adjusted—or didn't?
   Did it affect how your message was received?
   How did it affect you—your energy, clarity, or sense of authenticity?
4 **Strategize Moving Forward**
   If you could do it again, what would you keep or change?
   How could you stay true to your message while staying strategic?
5 **Talk It Out**
   Share your reflection with a trusted colleague.
   How do you each manage the tension between being direct and being strategic?
   How can you support each other in holding the line?

## Conflict as a Leadership Tool

Conflict isn't the enemy of progress. Complacency is. Yet many leadership structures, especially those shaped by white normative culture, treat conflict as something to be avoided rather than a force for change. Difficult conversations often get deferred, softened, or framed as disruptive, especially when they challenge the comfort of those in power. This instinct to preserve harmony doesn't create stability; it preserves the status quo, dictating which conversations are permissible and whose discomfort is prioritized. And often, what's framed as a desire for harmony is a demand for comfort, which is itself a form of privilege. Real stability comes from facing tensions directly, not avoiding them.

For leaders committed to equity, avoiding conflict isn't an option. Equity leaders must anticipate resistance, recognize coded language ("not a team player," "too emotional"), and redirect the conversation toward the real issue: dismantling barriers to justice. Calls for harmony and consensus are often weaponized to suppress necessary critique. For example, when an assistant principal raised concerns about the lack of representation in the school's advanced courses, pointing out that Black and Latinx students were significantly underrolled, a colleague responded, "We need to be careful not to accuse people. Everyone here supports kids." Rather than backing down, the assistant principal refocused the conversation on the data and asked, "This isn't about assigning blame. I'm trying to understand why certain students are underrepresented in these spaces and what structural changes we need to make to shift that." Effective leaders counter these tactics by shifting the focus from personal comfort to systemic impact. Conflict, when wielded well, can be a clarifying force. It can be a tool for justice rather than a barrier to it.

This next activity invites you to examine a moment when equity work was sidelined in the name of harmony. It helps you consider who was protected, who was left out, and how you might approach the situation differently next time, so your leadership stays grounded in impact, not just comfort.

>  **Activity: Shifting from Comfort to Impact**
>
> Step 1: Look Back
> Think of a time when you—or someone else—avoided conflict instead of addressing an equity issue.
>
> Ask yourself:
>
> - What was the equity concern?
> - Whose comfort or reputation got protected?
> - Who was left out, overlooked, or harmed?
>
> Step 2: Say What Was Missing
> Now rewrite what should have happened.
>
> - What needed to be named clearly?
> - What action or statement could have moved the conversation forward?
> - What would it have sounded like to prioritize impact over comfort?
>
> Step 3: Plan Ahead
> Decide what you'll do differently next time.
>
> - What will you say or do to stay focused on equity, even if it's uncomfortable?

## Managing Up, Down, and Sideways

Leadership is relational, but not all relationships carry the same weight, particularly in hierarchical institutions such as schools and districts. Patricia had to lead in all directions: up with Superintendent Leo, across with peer administrators, and down with principals, staff, and school communities. Each relationship required a different mix of clarity, strategy, and emotional labor. Research on adaptive leadership (Heifetz & Linsky, 2017) reminds us that leading for equity means navigating discomfort, not avoiding it. It means discerning where power resides, how resistance manifests, and who bears the risk when things become challenging.

In moments like this, it's easy to let the loudest voices set the narrative. Patricia reminded herself often: just because some staff were loud in their pushback didn't mean most were against building a more equitable school community. Some appreciated the clarity of the draft anti-racism policy. Other staff were uncertain, curious, or simply quiet, watching to see how leadership would respond. Letting vocal dissent dictate the pace would be a mistake. Change succeeds by mobilizing the willing, rather than appeasing the most resistant (Gorski & Swalwell, 2024). That's where leaders need to focus their energy.

Adaptive leadership also teaches us that resistance is often a response to perceived loss: loss of control, identity, familiarity, or status. When people resist equity efforts, it's rarely about the specific strategy. It's usually about what they fear they'll have to give up. For example, when a school shifts from zero-tolerance discipline to a more relationship-based, skill-building approach, some staff may fear losing authority or worry that student behavior will spiral. The job of the leader isn't to avoid that resistance, but to manage it with discipline and direction, acknowledging the discomfort while staying anchored in the goal of creating a more inclusive, responsive, and equitable school environment.

Managing up requires clarity, courage, and strategic alignment. When a district leader sees that equity work is being sidelined or scapegoated, managing up means naming the stakes clearly: If we continue to sidestep hard truths, racial and language disparities, the invisibility of entire student groups, inconsistent access to supports, we're not just failing students. We're inviting legal exposure, undermining trust with families, and weakening the integrity of our stated values.

That message must be delivered without defensiveness or apology. This is how equity leaders draw a line: by grounding their stance in the institution's priorities, like student outcomes, safety, and public accountability, and making it clear that delaying or diluting efforts toward equity jeopardizes all of them.

Managing up also means holding senior leaders accountable for their role in publicly supporting and protecting the equity efforts they lead. If a process misstep, such as the premature release of a policy draft, sparks controversy, equity leaders must not be left to absorb the fallout alone. Proper support includes stepping forward, acknowledging missteps, and taking visible ownership. If equity is a district value, leadership must reflect that openly and prominently. Before the error, the superintendent could have introduced the antiracism policy draft as an important and evolving initiative, framing it as a collaborative effort with staff, students, and families. When the draft was mistakenly released early, the superintendent could have immediately clarified that the premature circulation was an internal error, not a failure of the equity initiative itself. He could have affirmed the district's commitment to finalizing the policy through an inclusive and intentional process, thereby protecting both the integrity of the effort and the credibility of those leading it.

Managing across involves navigating peer influence, different personalities, comfort levels, and varying levels of commitment among colleagues. The goal is not to win over every critic. Instead, equity leaders should focus on identifying allies, building momentum with those who are ready, and strategically disengaging from relationships that repeatedly stall progress.

Start with the willing. Invite them to co-lead initiatives, share credit, and increase their visibility. Not only does this distribute ownership, but it also helps normalize the pursuit of equity across the organization. For those on the fence, lead with curiosity. Ask questions that surface their concerns without heightening resistance: What support would make this feel more doable? What impact are you most worried about? For those who've shown a persistent unwillingness to engage, stop chasing. Energy spent on resistant actors often yields little. Progress shifts when the work speaks for itself.

Managing down, especially in the aftermath of controversy, requires re-grounding equity efforts with clarity and trust. Staff don't just need vision, they need to know the why, the how, and the what's next. In moments of resistance, don't retreat. Stay visible. Host small-group listening sessions across grade levels, not to defend your position, but to re-engage people in the process. Ask: What's coming up for you? What would support look like? What still feels unclear?

Effective leaders in these moments don't soften the message; they build shared ownership. As Elena Aguilar reminds us in The *Art of Coaching Teams* (2016) and more recently in *Coaching for Equity* (2020), people trust leaders who show up with steadiness, emotional presence, and clarity even when the path is messy. When the backlash is loud, remember volume isn't the same as majority opinion. Often, the most vocal resistance comes from a small group of individuals. Many staff are watching and waiting to see how leadership responds. Strategic equity leaders learn to distinguish between voices that require engagement and those that require boundaries, and they lead accordingly.

Use the activity below to assess where you are spending your energy and how to lead more strategically in your sphere of influence.

---

 **Activity: Mapping Where to Spend Your Energy**

Decide how to lead more strategically in one key relationship—so your time and energy align with your values and goals.

### Step 1: Name the Relationship
Choose one person you work with—this could be someone you manage, a peer, or someone with more authority.

### Step 2: Reflect Honestly
Ask yourself:

- Are they open to change or mostly protecting the status quo?
- When I engage with them, does it move the work forward, or drain energy?
- If I pulled back, what would happen?

> **Step 3: Choose Your Strategy**
> Based on your reflection, decide:
>
> - Should I lean in and build?
> - Should I push more directly?
> - Should I step back and shift my focus?
>
> **Step 4: Take One Action**
> What's one thing you'll do differently in this relationship this week?

## Preparing for the Superintendent Conversation: Naming Non-Negotiables and Understanding Consequences

When I met with Patricia to prepare for her upcoming meeting with the superintendent, we focused on sharpening her message. She wanted to stay grounded, keep the focus on institutional accountability, and resist being pulled into defending her tone or managing staff discomfort.

The dynamics were layered. Patricia understood that Leo, the superintendent, faced political pressure and internal complexity. But he also held positional power, and with it, the responsibility to lead. Patricia needed to engage his power without getting swept into his politics.

Effective relationship management, navigating conflict, influencing others, and holding people accountable while maintaining clarity and purpose requires a willingness to name what matters most. Knowing your non-negotiables and being honest about the risks of naming them is essential. Otherwise, it's too easy to fall into the trap of preserving surface-level harmony instead of driving change.

So first, I asked Patricia to name her non-negotiables:

- The work couldn't be diluted to protect comfort.

- The conversation had to stay focused on the work, rather than on how people perceived her.
- If there were concerns, they needed to be named directly, not filtered through coded language or intermediaries.
- And, importantly, Leo would need to own publicly and support the antiracism policy, rather than letting her absorb the fallout alone.

I asked, "What would success look like in this conversation?"

She didn't hesitate. "I need him to stop deflecting. Every time this work is challenged, it's reframed as a process issue: the pace is too fast, people aren't ready, we need more buy-in. But none of those names the resistance. If there are real concerns, I want him to say them directly to me. I need to know if he's truly committed, or if I'm being asked to play politics. I need him to say equity is non-negotiable. That we're not debating if it's a priority, only how we move it forward. And I need him to take public responsibility for the rollout mistake. Mollie shared the draft prematurely. That was her error. I've taken all the heat for it, and he's been silent. If he wants staff to trust this work, he has to own it, publicly. That includes defending its intent, not just diffusing tension."

"And if he won't?" I asked.

She didn't flinch. "Then I need to know. If I'm expected to soften, slow down, or play the 'reasonable middle' between equity and resistance, I need to be clear: that's not leadership. That's not the work I'm interested in. I did not accept this job to make people feel better about avoiding change."

I asked her to consider the potential consequences of naming all this.

She began to count: "One: He could decide I'm the problem. That I'm too much, too fast, too disruptive. Two: He could nod along but still let pushback dictate the pace. Three: This could get political. The school committee already monitors this work as if it were a liability. If he frames it as 'Patricia wants to go faster, but I'm balancing the politics,' I become the reckless one. He gets to be the reasonable one. Four: He could start laying the groundwork to push me out. Maybe not today, but eventually. I've seen it happen."

I asked, "Can you live with those risks?"

She nodded. "Yeah. I'm done guessing. And I'm done being second-guessed. I know my worth. I'm going to get an answer."

## Framing the Conversation with Radical Candor

Kim Scott's Radical Candor framework, which comprises two key components—challenging directly while caring personally—offers useful guidance in equity leadership, but only if you're realistic about how power, race, and role shape the reception of candor.

Equity conversations require directness. The pursuit of justice is too urgent, the harm too real, for coded language or excessive politeness. Radical Candor, in theory, is about naming the truth in service of shared growth. However, in practice, especially in institutions such as schools, where hierarchy and identity politics influence perception, directness can be a double-edged sword. When a superintendent challenges a principal, it's likely perceived as a demonstration of accountability. When a director challenges a superintendent, it may be perceived as "pushback." When a Black woman leader names inequity plainly, it is often perceived as "divisive" or "aggressive." This approach carries risks, especially for those who are already under scrutiny. Research on the glass cliff phenomenon (Ryan, Haslam, & Rink, 2022) highlights how women, particularly women of color, are often appointed to leadership roles during times of crisis, only to be blamed when transformation proves challenging. Being direct in those situations can pose a real risk: necessary for change, but an easy way to be labeled "too much" or "the problem."

This is why preparing for conversations like Patricia's requires more than rehearsing talking points. It requires clarifying your values, naming what you won't walk back from, and anticipating how your truth-telling will be received. It also means asking for action, not just acknowledgement.

In this case, Patricia's radical candor would include:

- Naming the superintendent's silence as a risk to the work.
- Asking him to take visible responsibility for the premature policy release.
- Requesting that he publicly affirm the district's commitment to anti-racism, clearly and without apology.

While challenging others is always a part of equity leadership, another important part is deciding how much of yourself you're willing to offer to keep equity efforts honest. Radical Candor can be a helpful framework, but only when the conditions are honest and the consequences acknowledged. For equity leaders who don't hold the final decision-making power, the key is to be forceful without becoming the scapegoat and strategic without diluting the message. That means:

- Naming the work as a shared commitment, not a personal crusade.
- Refusing triangulation, insisting on direct conversations with stakeholders instead of working through intermediaries.
- Linking equity to institutional survival and making clear that ignoring inequities creates more significant risks than addressing them.

While it is not easy or certain, it is possible to push without alienating, challenge without being sidelined, and hold leadership accountable without making yourself disposable. It is possible to speak truth to power and ensure that the truth leads to action.

## The Superintendent Conversation

Patricia walked into Leo's office ready to lead with clarity and emotional steadiness. She had replayed their last conversation too many times. This one had to be different.

**Patricia:** I want to start by acknowledging the immense pressure everyone is under right now. I know principals and staff are holding a lot, and I don't take that lightly. You also know how deeply committed I am to our students and families. From the beginning, we agreed that equity wouldn't be a side initiative. It would be central to how we lead as a district. That was the shared commitment, and that's why I came here.

    Our last conversation left me confused. For nearly two years, I've led this work in alignment with the priorities we agreed on. You never told me to slow down—not once. Then, suddenly, I hear that the staff have been saying this for a while and that I need to show more patience. That feedback would have been helpful much earlier. I'm naming that now because I don't want to walk into this conversation unsure of where we stand.

**Leo:** Patricia, you've done important work. However, there's no denying the intense reaction to that draft. Staff are saying the rollout was mishandled. Some feel blamed. The leadership team's shaken. We need to stabilize before we move again.

**Patricia:** I'm not dismissing how people felt when they read the draft. However, I want to ensure we're not confusing their discomfort with harm. Discomfort can be part of growth, especially in equity work. And honestly, what shook me was how quickly the focus shifted from the mistake in process to questioning the work itself.

**Leo:** I can see that. I'll be honest—I wasn't expecting the level of heat we got. Some of it surprised me. And I didn't handle that moment as well as I should have.

**Patricia:** I appreciate you saying that. And I'm naming this not because I want to litigate the past, but because I need us to be on the same page if we're moving forward. Silence, in moments like that, is often interpreted as a retreat. And I was left holding it all—fielding questions, absorbing frustration, trying to steady a message I didn't control.

**Leo:** That's fair. I didn't mean to put you in that position, but I can see how it happened. It was a scramble. I was trying to keep things from escalating further. It wasn't fair how I put all this on you.

**Patricia:** Thank you for saying that. We can learn from having missed an opportunity to lead through the crisis. When people don't hear clearly from leadership that we stand behind the intent of the work, then the loudest voices get to write the story. And that's dangerous—for our credibility, and for the students and families who already feel unseen.

**Leo:** You're right about that. I let the noise steer me. And I didn't realize how much that left you exposed. I'm still catching up to the impact that moment had.

**Patricia:** I'd like to shift to what's next and how we move forward. People need clarity now. And that clarity has to come from you. Staff need to hear that the policy was shared prematurely, yes, but that the district still stands behind the intent and the need for this work. Because if they don't hear that, the message is: we weren't that serious about equity and antiracism work in the first place. Staff need to know that our equity commitments are still in effect and that you are willing to confirm this publicly.

**Leo:** You are right. This has been on my mind too. I'll think about how to address the miscommunication.

**Patricia:** You'll think about it?

**Leo:** I'll address the miscommunication.

**Patricia:** To be clear, does that mean staff will hear that equity is a top priority, that the policy was shared in error, and that you stand behind its intent and me in leading a collaborative process that includes staff, students, and families?

**Leo:** Yes. Staff will hear that. Since you're clear on what needs to be said, why don't you draft the communication plan for my review?

**Patricia:** Absolutely. Once your message is sent out, I can reinforce the purpose of the work, hold space for feedback, and coach staff through the process; however, your public stance sets the foundation. That's how we stabilize.

**Leo:** I hope there's no new fallout from this.

**Patricia:** The conversation is already happening—on social media, in community spaces, in staff rooms. Families are watching. Students are watching. And so are the staff who are ready for this work, waiting to see if we'll follow through. If we don't follow through, the real harm will fall on the students and families who have always been overlooked—those whose needs this policy was meant to address. If we walk away now, we tell them, once again, that their value is negotiable.

**Leo:** I already said I'm with you. Please provide me with the statement by the end of the day. Let's meet this week—just the two of us—and map out a careful path forward.

Patricia walked out with a calendar invite and a possible opening. But she knew better than to mistake his acquiescence for a real commitment. She needed to see that he was going to take the lead on the work and stand beside her when the pressure came. Because next time, she wouldn't carry it alone.

The activity below will help you prepare for the kinds of conversations equity leaders face every day: the ones where staying firm, clear, and strategic makes all the difference.

---

 **Activity: Holding the Line—Preparing for High-Stakes Conversations**

Step 1: Identify Your Core Message
What do you need to say? Write it in one or two clear sentences.

Step 2: Name Why It Matters
What harm continues if you stay silent? Who benefits if you speak up?

Write one sentence to remind yourself of that.

Step 3: Anticipate Pushback
What resistance are you likely to hear?

- "People aren't ready."
- "That language is too harsh."
- "Now's not the time."

Step 4: Plan Your Response
What will you say that brings the focus back to impact, not discomfort?

Write one sentence to re-center the conversation on responsibility, not reactions.

Step 5: Say It Out Loud
Practice saying your message and your response to pushback. Practice with a colleague.

## Final Thoughts

One of the most persistent challenges in equity work is the belief that it must always feel good to be effective. When Patricia pushed for change, she often heard the same refrains: *Can't we make it more positive? Can't it feel less 'us vs. them'?* These questions may sound like calls for unity, but more often, they are requests to soften the truth to preserve comfort, especially for those in power. But meaningful movement almost always comes with discomfort.

Schools often expect conversations about injustice to be carefully worded to avoid upsetting anyone. If the tone is right—urgent but not too urgent, clear but not too unsettling—people will get on board. When people ask for a "more positive" tone or a conversation that feels "less divisive," they often attempt to discuss inequity without confronting the power structures that uphold it. Avoiding that confrontation only delays change. And that delay has a cost, especially for students and staff who live with the inequities.

This is the reality of equity leadership: people will trip up. They will get defensive, fall back on old patterns, and sometimes even retreat from personal and institutional change entirely when the pressure mounts. Superintendents, like the one Patricia works with, may buckle under political pressure or opt for safer ground in the moment. That's human. But it's also why the work requires more than intention. It requires accountability. And that responsibility often falls on the shoulders of the equity leader.

Patricia and other equity leaders like her don't just advance equity efforts. They hold others to it. That's the added burden: not just pushing for institutional change, but also pulling others along with them, including those with more positional power. They're expected to be strategists, emotional buffers, truth-tellers, and diplomats. And when things get hard, and they always do, the burden of "how to say it" often falls solely on the shoulders of equity leaders.

This is why equity work can't rest on one person, no matter how skilled or committed they may be. It must be shared and supported at every level, especially at the top. Without institutional support and deep self-examination from all leaders, equity becomes a side initiative—something to manage rather than a responsibility to own.

None of this means advancing equity has to be hostile or punitive. But it *does* have to be honest, and honesty is not always comfortable. The real question isn't whether equity work will create discomfort but whether leaders will sit with that discomfort, stay with it, and move through it long enough to make real change.

### Bringing it Back to You

◆ Where do you see yourself in relationship management? Which dynamics—managing up, down, or sideways—challenge you the most, and why?

- How do you handle the tension between persistence and strategy? Have you ever softened your message to gain buy-in? What was the result?
- What role does conflict play in your leadership? Do you tend to avoid, embrace, or manage it selectively? How does this impact your work?
- When have you chosen to disengage strategically? How did that choice serve or limit your ability to create change?
- How can you hold leaders accountable? What would it look like in your role?

### *Bringing it Back to Your Team*

- Are we prioritizing relationships over change? Where do we see the politics of palatability at play in our organization?
- How do we handle conflict? Do we encourage honest conversations or default to comfort and consensus?
- Where is equity positioned in our leadership? Is it central to decision-making, or is it treated as an initiative that needs careful management?
- Who do we listen to, and who do we dismiss? Are we allowing certain voices to shape our direction while marginalizing others?
- How do we define commitment? What does true investment in equity work look like, and how do we hold each other accountable?

# 7

# Responsible Decision-Making

> **Big Ideas in This Chapter**
>
> ◆ Every decision a leader makes either protects the status quo or shifts it. Silence, ambiguity, and deflection are also decisions, and they often perpetuate harm.
> ◆ Ethical leadership means choosing people over politics. It requires naming inequity, responding to harm in real time, and refusing to treat student safety as optional.
> ◆ Moral courage is a leadership practice. It's built over time by making hard calls, holding to your purpose, and staying aligned with what matters—even when there's something to lose.
> ◆ Institutions don't change just because leaders mean well. They change when leaders act differently, when they stay accountable even when no one is watching.

Have you ever made a decision that felt smart in the moment, practical, efficient, maybe necessary, only to realize later that it sent the wrong message or caused unintended harm? Leadership is full of those moments. Responsible decision-making doesn't mean we have all the answers. It means we stay grounded in our purpose and values when the pressure is high and the path isn't clear.

This chapter brings together the inner and outer work explored so far—self-awareness, self-management, social awareness, and relationship management—and applies these concepts to one of the most challenging aspects of leadership: doing the right thing when it comes at a personal cost. When equity is at stake, good intentions won't carry the weight. What matters is what you choose, how you follow through, and who you're willing to hold accountable, including yourself.

Because in the end, culture isn't shaped by what you say you believe. It's shaped by what you do when it counts.

## Case Study: Edison Middle School

Edison Middle School sits in a district that once prided itself on inclusive values, but over the past few years, the ground has shifted. The superintendent, who has been in the position for less than three years, has already announced that he will resign at the end of the year, his departure shadowed by mounting political pressure and public controversy. Two Directors of Diversity, Equity, and Inclusion have also stepped down—the second leaving abruptly after receiving targeted threats, an event that rattled staff and signaled just how hostile the situation had become.

The school board, once a quiet procedural body, is now dominated by a slim majority aligned with a "parents' rights" coalition. Their platform has included efforts to ban certain books, question LGBTQ+ inclusion efforts, and restrict what they call "political symbols" in classrooms, like Black Lives Matter posters and Pride flags. Board meetings have become contentious spectacles, livestreamed with hostile comment sections and polarizing talking points.

At Edison, Principal Whitaker is doing everything she can to maintain stability at the school. She's in her 12th year as principal and has deep roots in the district, as a teacher, assistant principal, and parent, and is just two years from retirement. She's built trust across lines of difference, and students gravitate toward her calm presence and clear sense of care. She was the one who formalized stipends for affinity group sponsors and encouraged staff to create spaces where students could see themselves reflected. She's used to being applauded for her efforts, and she's never had to navigate this level of scrutiny or fear.

Jordan is a seventh grader at Edison—quick-witted, social, and known for making their classmates (and teachers) laugh at just the right moment. They're confident in class discussions, especially when topics spark debate, and they bring a sharp sense of humor to group projects. At the start of the school year, Jordan shared that they identify as nonbinary and use they/them pronouns. While a few teachers stumbled early on, most made an effort. But in the halls, things were different. It started with deliberate misgendering and small snickers. Then, one afternoon in the cafeteria, a group of boys filmed Jordan while mocking their appearance and voice. The video was shared in a private group chat labeled "freakshow." Within hours, it had circulated across much of the seventh grade.

Jordan reported the video to the assistant principal, who promised to "handle it appropriately." But there was no follow-up with Jordan. When Jordan's parents called, they were told disciplinary action had been taken but weren't given any specifics. Jordan now avoids the bathroom at school, skips lunch, and has started asking to stay home from school. Whitaker didn't find out until two weeks later, when Jordan's mother emailed her directly. She was shocked. She called the family immediately, listened to them, and apologized. She pulled her team together, tried to piece together what had happened, and realized that her leadership team wasn't functioning as well as she had trusted.

At the same time, a parent's complaint about a Pride flag in Ms. Alston's eighth-grade English class landed on her desk. The parent claimed the flag was "confusing" and "political," and questioned the teacher's intentions. That same evening, a cropped photo of the classroom wall appeared on a community Facebook group, with hundreds of comments accusing the school of "indoctrination." District leadership said nothing publicly but sent an internal memo the next day advising principals to "pause" all classroom displays not explicitly tied to curriculum standards. Teachers are looking to Whitaker for direction. Some have quietly taken down posters, flags, and safe space stickers. Other staff refuse.

Whitaker walks the halls every morning, as she has always done, checking in on students and trying to maintain a sense of normalcy. She still smiles, still notices when someone's head is down, still asks teachers how their day is going. But inside, she's reckoning with her own doubts.

She's two years from retirement. She's seen what happens to people who speak too loudly or stand too firmly. No one showed up for them when the pressure mounted. Whitaker wants to support her students. She means that. She knows what the Pride flag and signs meant to Jordan and LGBTQ+ students. She knows the district's vague directive to "pause displays" is code for "take it down before it becomes a headline." And she knows that resisting could put her in the spotlight—emails, calls, screenshots, boardroom drama.

She has explicitly told me she doesn't want to be tomorrow's news. She doesn't want her final years in education reduced to damage control or scandal. She's still trying to find another way through, one that protects her students without sacrificing herself. But each day, the line she's walking feels thinner. And the question echoing in her mind—How do I lead with care and still survive this?—has no easy answer.

## Responsible Decision-Making as the Embodiment of the Ideal Self

As we read in Chapter 3, Richard Boyatzis's Intentional Change Theory (2006) posits that meaningful, lasting change starts with a clear vision of the ideal self, the leader one aspires to be. But that vision is meaningless if it collapses under pressure. Responsible decision-making is where leaders either live out their values or default to habits shaped by fear, self-preservation, or the status quo. It's where leadership moves from aspiration to action, or inaction.

Principal Whitaker has that vision. She's spent decades building a reputation as someone who cares deeply for her students and staff, someone who believes that schools should be places where young people feel safe, seen, and valued. But now, she finds herself in a district where public commitment to equity work has withered, and the costs of standing firm are painfully clear. She's not imagining the risk.

This is the tension at the heart of responsible decision-making in equity leadership: the difference between who we want to be and what we're willing to risk to be that person. But the ideal self must be more than a professional branding statement; it must be durable enough to withstand fear, fragile relationships, and institutional ambiguity. Responsible decision-making is where the rubber meets the road. It is not a matter of moral clarity alone, but of strategy and courage.

Whitaker's dilemma is one that, unfortunately, all equity leaders face: *What can I protect without losing my job? How much can I say before I become the story?* These questions don't make her weak or hypocritical; they make her human. Still, leadership rooted in intentional change means acknowledging those tensions and choosing actions that keep the ideal self in view, not just when it's easy, but also when it's risky.

Boyatzis's theory holds that intentional change happens in relationships, not isolation. But Whitaker is increasingly alone. The district has gone quiet. Her leadership team struggles with follow-through. Staff are afraid. Families are watching. In this moment, the question is not whether she knows what the right thing is. It's whether she can do it without enough support around her to steady the cost. And if she can't do it alone, what would it take to build that support before the next decision comes? For Whitaker, as for many leaders, the decisions ahead of her are not only about Jordan, or the flag, or the district's silence. They are about whether she can hold onto the leader she set out to be, even when the system makes that feel almost impossible.

## The Role of Identity, Bias, and Fear in Leadership Decision-Making

Responsible decision-making doesn't happen in a vacuum. It is filtered through a leader's own lived experience, social identity, implicit biases, and very real fears about personal and professional consequences. What one leader sees as a necessary act to protect students, another may perceive as an unnecessary risk. In equity work, the stakes of those perceptions can't be overstated.

Research on implicit bias (Gullo & Beachum, 2020) indicates that even well-intentioned individuals may unconsciously favor dominant narratives when under pressure, particularly in ambiguous situations. In school leadership, this plays out when leaders hesitate to act decisively on issues involving race, gender identity, or other marginalized identities out of fear of community backlash, reputational harm, or job security. Fear of public scrutiny, of being labeled "political," of becoming the target, can narrow the field of vision, making inaction feel safer than confronting injustice.

This is evident not only in Whitaker's story but in schools across the country. In one district, a principal declined to intervene when teachers repeatedly misgendered a trans student, citing the need to "respect all viewpoints." In another instance, a superintendent halted a district-wide ethnic studies pilot after a handful of vocal parents called it "anti-American," despite the program having already increased student engagement and attendance in its early stages. In both cases, leaders allowed fear and political pressure, not student needs or equity commitments, to define what was "reasonable" or "responsible."

Years ago, at a school I led, families discovered there was a plan for fracking trucks operated by the politically connected property development company to pass by our school, potentially releasing toxic chemicals. This was both an environmental issue and an equity issue. Fracking trucks don't pass through wealthy neighborhoods. They run through working-class, multilingual, and historically marginalized communities like ours, where resistance is assumed to be minimal. Research confirms that low-income communities and communities of color are disproportionately exposed to environmental hazards due to systemic disinvestment and structural racism (Taylor, 2020).

When I shared this concern with our board, a member employed by the company told me, in front of everyone, to shut my mouth and stay out of a white-hot, divisive issue I knew nothing about. Some board members apologized to me privately, and one offered to "have drinks" with him to smooth it over, saying his comments "didn't reflect who we are." But they did. No one publicly challenged what he said. No one stood beside me. When I refused to attend the next meeting without both a clear resolution and accountability for what had happened, several board members resigned, claiming they had joined the board to support children, not to engage in conflict. Protecting political relationships took precedence over protecting students or leading in solidarity. Responsible decision-making requires leaders to act even when doing so threatens access, approval, or comfort. Equity can't survive leadership that folds under pressure. This kind of retreat reveals how political self-protection often gets mislabeled as neutrality or care, when in reality, it sustains harm.

According to the Equity Literacy Framework (Gorski & Swalwell, 2023), equity-literate leaders must be able to recognize even subtle forms of inequity, respond in ways that disrupt those patterns, and redress harm with urgency. But that work can't happen if leaders interpret safety through the lens of political survival. Equity decisions often bring discomfort, social, political, even professional, but discomfort is not the same as danger. For students harmed by silence, the danger is real. Responsible leadership requires the courage and skill to distinguish between discomfort and harm, between what is easy and what is right.

## Institutional Silence and the Psychology of Safety

Institutional silence, when leaders or systems fail to speak or act clearly in the face of harm, sends a powerful message: *this is not a place where you are protected.* For students with historically marginalized identities, that silence often speaks louder than the harm itself. It creates uncertainty about whether their experiences will be acknowledged, validated, or repaired. Over time, it conditions them to expect neither justice nor safety.

This kind of ambiguity, where harm is met with vague assurances, delayed responses, or procedural deflection, has real psychological and academic consequences. Claude Steele's reflections (Steele, 2021) on stereotype threat and the related concept of belonging uncertainty (Walton & Cohen, 2011) help us understand why. When students question whether they belong, whether they will be judged through the lens of a stereotype, or whether their identities put them at risk, they often experience chronic stress, disengagement, and diminished performance. The threat isn't just the individual incident; it's the institutional response to that incident. When schools fail to name and respond to identity-based harm, students are left wondering: *Is this what happens here? Is anyone going to say something?*

Take Jordan. After being filmed and mocked by peers, the response from Edison Middle School was tepid at best. The students who targeted them faced no visible consequences. Jordan received no meaningful follow-up. The lack of a clear, public response made it worse, not only for Jordan but for every LGBTQ+ student who saw what happened and quietly recalculated what it meant to be visible. The Pride flag controversy sent a similar signal. By "pausing" displays instead of defending them, the district implied that students' safety was conditional and expendable.

This doesn't apply only to students. Amy Edmondson's work on psychological safety (Edmondson, 2023) shows that adults, too, become less likely to speak up or take risks in environments where the consequences for doing so are unclear or inconsistent. In schools, this is evident when staff witness harm but hesitate to intervene because they're unsure whether leadership will support them or leave them vulnerable. When values are implied but not enacted, trust begins to erode.

In one district, a school counselor was told not to run a support group for LGBTQ+ students because it might "alienate families." In another, a middle school principal removed a display honoring Arab American Heritage Month after a single parent's complaint, despite overwhelming support from students and staff. Elsewhere, a district leader asked a teacher to remove the "Black Lives Matter" sign from her classroom wall, citing concerns that it could be "politically divisive." These aren't anomalies. They're examples of how institutions perpetuate inequity through avoidance, erasure, and misplaced caution, illustrating how silence and ambiguity serve as institutional patterns that protect some at the expense of other groups.

To be clear: silence doesn't just fail to stop harm, it sustains it. Leaders may believe that staying neutral avoids escalation, but in practice, it often escalates harm for the people most affected. Equity work isn't about passive empathy or quiet support. It's about having the skill and will to recognize, respond to, and redress inequity in real time (Gorski & Swalwell, 2023). Responsible decision-making means naming what we would rather ignore, not just because it's ethically right, but because it's necessary for belonging, trust, and safety to take root. Schools thrive when their values are lived, not just stated, when students and staff can count on action, not ambiguity.

## Adaptive Leadership and the Myth of Neutrality

Some leadership challenges have clear solutions. Other challenges demand a shift in mindset, relationships, and culture. This distinction between technical problems and adaptive challenges (Brown, 2023) underscores the need for leaders to engage in adaptive work that involves changing values, beliefs, roles, and approaches. Technical problems can be addressed through procedural fixes or expert assistance. Adaptive challenges, however, require people, often whole institutions, to learn new ways of thinking and acting. They demand discomfort, courage, and long-term cultural work.

Identity-based harm is an adaptive challenge. It is not resolved by "pausing" announcements, taking down flags, or issuing neutral statements. Those are technical responses to a deeply adaptive problem. When Edison Middle responded to parent complaints about a Pride flag by quietly removing it without explanation or affirmation, the district didn't neutralize the issue; it shifted the burden of discomfort from the system onto students like Jordan and educators trying to create inclusive spaces. The harm persisted and became increasingly insidious.

Neutrality, especially in response to harm, is not a morally neutral position. As Kendi (2019) reminds us, "The opposite of 'racist' isn't 'not racist.' It's antiracist." In equity work, the same logic applies. The opposite of injustice isn't polite silence, it's action. Sensoy and DiAngelo (2017) argue that when leaders aim to remain neutral in the face of inequity, they're not avoiding politics; they're enacting a political choice that benefits dominant groups by protecting the status quo. Silence doesn't soothe, it solidifies imbalance.

Adaptive leadership requires something more. It requires recognizing that people will resist the discomfort of change and understanding that resistance to change is not a setback, but rather evidence that deeper work is needed. Effective adaptive leaders create environments where discomfort is expected and used as a catalyst for growth (Brown, 2023). Instead of smoothing over tension, adaptive leaders surface it, confront underlying power dynamics, and anchor the work in clear values, even when the risks are real.

Equity leaders understand that equity doesn't live in a single decision; it lives in *how* decisions ripple through systems and relationships. So the critical question becomes: *Whose discomfort are we managing, and whose safety are we sacrificing?* If a district removes a Pride flag to avoid upsetting parents, what message does it send to students whose identities are constantly debated? If a school leader avoids naming racism after an incident, what does it teach staff about what's permissible to ignore? Equity-centered leadership requires naming those trade-offs out loud and refusing to pretend that silence is neutral. The goal is not to create harmony by avoiding harm; it's to create justice by disrupting it. And that work is always adaptive. It cannot be delegated. It cannot be avoided.

## Transparency, Repair, and Communal Accountability

In equity-centered leadership, decision-making is more than making the "right" call—it includes how that call is communicated, how harm is acknowledged, and how relationships are rebuilt. When harm has occurred, especially identity-based harm, the community is watching not just for resolution, but for recognition. Silence or vagueness may initially reduce conflict, but it erodes trust over time. Transparent leadership shows people that their pain is seen and that your values remain steady, even in the storm.

This is where the idea of *institutional repair* becomes essential. Drawing on truth and reconciliation processes and the evolving concept of moral repair in political philosophy, institutional repair entails acknowledging past harm, taking ownership, and committing to a continuous process that centers on the voices and needs of those who have been affected (Gobodo-Madikizela, 2024). It's often the missing piece in school systems that respond to equity challenges with behind-closed-doors management.

Institutional repair starts when leaders stop trying to manage optics and start owning the harm. What happened at Edison Middle School wasn't just a misstep. It was a failure of protection. A student was publicly harassed for their identity. The response from school leadership was delayed, vague, and ultimately incomplete. The students responsible were not meaningfully held accountable. Signs came down with no explanation. And students like Jordan got the message: *you're on your own.*

Repair requires more than words. It demands direct, comprehensive action. What might this look like? Whitaker and I sketched out a course of action, one that acknowledged the harm publicly, took ownership without defensiveness, and committed to sustained changes shaped by the voices of those most impacted.

First, the leadership team needs to acknowledge what happened publicly. That means naming, without hiding behind legalese or euphemism, that a student was targeted for being LGBTQ+, and that the school's initial response didn't live up to its stated values. This isn't to shame individuals, but to restore credibility.

Second, the students who caused the harm need to be held accountable in a manner that is both educational and disciplinary. It's not enough to say "they were talked to." That approach protects the system, not the student. Accountability should include required participation in learning about gender identity, bias, and the real-world impact of discriminatory behavior. Students responsible for harm should also contribute to institutional efforts to strengthen safety and belonging for all students. If restorative dialogue is considered, it must only occur if the harmed student chooses it, at their discretion and their own pace. Authentic restoration focuses not just on interpersonal repair but on rebuilding the broader institutional conditions of trust, safety, and inclusion that were damaged.

Third, the school must address the broader community with honesty and ownership. LGBTQ+ students should not be asked to relive their harm or do the emotional labor of repairing trust. That burden belongs to leadership and those with institutional power. Facilitated conversations should confront the conditions that allowed harm, rather than gathering stories from students with marginalized identities. For example, staff may be required to engage in critical learning about bias and institutional complicity, rather than just offering apologies. Anonymous surveys should be used to expose the realities of safety and belonging, and the results must lead to immediate, public changes. Leadership must stop treating harm as an isolated incident and begin treating it as evidence of deeper institutional failure.

As Gorski and Swalwell (2021) emphasize in their Equity Literacy Framework, responding to inequity is not enough; institutions must also redress it by dismantling the conditions that allowed the harm to occur. Equity commitments must be updated visibly, backed by action, and tied directly to how leadership and staff are evaluated, for example, by incorporating equity goals and measures of cultural competence into performance reviews. True repair does not respond to one event; it transforms the policies, practices, and leadership behaviors that made the harm possible.

Ultimately, the leadership team must take responsibility for the harm caused by removing visible symbols of inclusion. The Pride flag wasn't a random decoration; it was a signal of safety. Taking it down sent a clear message, whether intended or not. If that decision was made out of fear, that needs to be named. If it was made under district pressure, that too should be said aloud. Either way, the flag should be raised again, accompanied by a clear explanation of its meaning and the importance of visibility. And if district policy is unclear, the school should advocate publicly for a policy that aligns with its stated values.

None of this is about grand gestures. It's about being honest. Repair means identifying what went wrong, addressing not just the individual missteps but the deeper institutional failures that allowed harm to occur, and implementing changes that transform the culture. If a school is serious about equity, then silence, delay, and watered-down accountability cannot be tolerated. Leadership must confront how its practices, norms, and inaction contributed to the harm and commit to changing them at their roots. Genuine healing and transformation require more than addressing individual acts of harm; they demand reimagining institutional culture to center on safety, equity, and collective well-being (Ginwright, 2022). This could involve overhauling reporting systems to track bias incidents transparently with clear consequences or embedding equity goals into school improvement plans. If leadership wants to rebuild trust, the only way forward is through a comprehensive, public, and sustained effort at repair, one that extends beyond apologies to encompass structural change.

Repair does not require us to be perfect. None of us can ever be that. However, it does mean telling the truth about what happened, clarifying the values that will guide the subsequent steps, and involving the community in envisioning a path forward. Leaders often avoid this level of transparency out of fear that it will deepen division. But done well, it creates the opposite: clarity, trust, and the possibility of healing.

## Final Thoughts: The Reality of the Work

Equity leadership may sound noble in theory, but in practice, it can be challenging, isolating, and even punishing. For Whitaker, that reality becomes undeniable in the months following Jordan's harassment and the district's quiet retreat from visible LGBTQ+ inclusion. The community is tense, the school board is watching, and the superintendent is silent. And yet, students and staff are still looking to her to show up, speak up, and lead.

Whitaker had developed many of the right skills. She was emotionally self-aware, able to manage her reactions effectively under pressure, and skilled at building strong, lasting relationships. She had worked to deepen her social awareness by listening carefully to staff and students, and creating space for student voice. She had even supported professional development on culturally responsive teaching and equity-driven practices. But in this moment, none of that translated into action.

Despite all the strategizing and planning for how to repair, Whitaker does what so many leaders do when the political risk becomes too great: she steps back. She tells herself she's protecting the school from backlash, protecting her staff from becoming targets. But she also knows she's protecting herself. The harm to students goes unaddressed.

This is where the limits of competency become clear. SEL skills are essential. They help leaders stay grounded, build trust, and engage in healthy conflict. But SEL is effective when paired with moral courage. It is not a substitute for it. Even the best-developed skill set cannot carry a leader through the most challenging moments if they're unwilling to act. Knowing what's right isn't enough. Leadership means acting on it, especially when it's hard.

Rushworth Kidder (2005) calls this kind of integrity in action *moral courage*: the willingness to stand up for what's right even when it's risky or uncomfortable. This is the part of equity leadership we often avoid naming—that sometimes, we choose our comfort over the values we claim to hold. Not because we don't have the skills, not because we don't care, but because we care more about blowback from staff, political pressure, lost credibility with peers, and even job security. So instead of confronting the issue, we sidestep. Instead of naming harm, we manage optics. That's how inequity survives. Sometimes it survives through overt opposition, but far more often through hesitation and silence. Through decisions that prioritize the status quo over accountability. Through leadership that says the right things but won't risk anything to act on them.

This is where moral courage becomes the defining trait of equity-centered leadership. Moral courage isn't the absence of fear; it's the decision to act through it. It's what's required of leaders when there's something real to lose: approval, influence, credibility, even a job. It's the choice to align your public leadership with your private conscience, even when it's inconvenient, unpopular, or professionally risky. It shouldn't have to cost this much. And yet it does. And as leaders, we must decide whether we're here to be complicit or to disrupt injustice.

Shawn Ginwright (2022) reminds us in his work on healing-centered leadership that equity work must involve personal reckoning—the inner work leaders must do to stay rooted in their purpose within systems that reward compliance over integrity. That reckoning is the foundation of moral courage. It allows leaders to act on their values, even when doing so comes at a cost. Moral courage is a leadership practice. It means telling the truth when it's easier not to, naming inequities even when no one else will, and making decisions that align with your values, especially under pressure. And it's not something you're born with. It's something you build.

You build it by getting clear on what you stand for. You strengthen it by practicing hard conversations. You sustain it by surrounding yourself with people who won't let you off the hook, because equity leadership will test you, not just once, but over and over again. Institutions change when leaders protect their people. You won't please everyone. You'll be called divisive, political, and too much.

Our most significant risk isn't in speaking up, it's in staying quiet while students are othered, families are excluded, and staff are left to navigate broken systems alone. So ask yourself: Who am I accountable to? What am I building? And when the stakes are high, when your credibility is questioned, when you're asked to choose between your values and your comfort, what will you do?

## *Bringing it Back to You*

- When have I recognized harm but hesitated to act? What influenced my decision?
- How do I distinguish between discomfort and real risk when making decisions?
- What values guide my leadership when no one is watching? Where do I struggle to hold that line?
- Who do I center in my decision-making—those most affected or those most likely to push back?
- What's one decision I need to revisit, name more clearly, or lead through more courageously?

## *Bringing it Back to Your Team*

- When harm happens, how do we respond as a team? Do we name it, delay it, or try to manage the optics?
- What messages do our decisions send about who belongs and what matters here?
- When has our team prioritized policy safety over student safety? How can we shift that balance?
- What support structures are in place for leaders or staff who speak up? What's missing?
- How do we build collective moral courage, not just good intentions, to make equity real?

# 8

# Putting It Into Practice
# A Reflection Tool for Equity-Centered Leadership

This chapter will help you translate the book's core ideas into tangible leadership practice. It offers a case study rooted in real challenges, where bias, avoidance, and discomfort must give way to responsibility and redress. It introduces a tool to help you reflect on your leadership. Together, they help bridge the social and emotional learning (SEL) competencies and leadership practices explored throughout the book, offering a pathway from reflection to meaningful action.

## Case Study

Drew, a middle school principal, was widely regarded for his commitment to antiracist leadership. A social studies teacher, Laila, had long felt uneasy about how the school handled religious and cultural differences. But it wasn't until a lunchtime incident during Ramadan that she raised her concerns. A student came to her in tears after being taunted by peers who waved food in her face and said things like, "Do you want to watch me eat this? Mmmmm," and "Why is your family starving you?" The student said it had happened before, but this time, she couldn't take it.

Laila met with Drew and shared broader concerns about how the school was failing its Muslim student population. Students observing Ramadan had repeatedly asked to eat in quiet spaces instead of the cafeteria, but were denied. Despite recognizing Yom Kippur and Good Friday, Eid al-Fitr was not included in the school calendar. Halal meal options were unavailable. Hijab-wearing students reported harassment that staff ignored. "I don't think anyone here is blatantly Islamophobic," Laila said, "but the school is most definitely Islamophobic."

Drew was jarred. He ended the conversation professionally, promising to come back to Laila, but knew he needed space to process what he'd heard.

Alone in his office, Drew felt the impact of the exchange: shaky hands, a tight chest, and a wave of embarrassment, defensiveness, and anger. His thoughts spiraled: *Doesn't she know how much I've done? This is district policy—how is this on me?* Then, beneath the resistance, fear. Fear that he had failed. Fear that his equity leadership was performative. And then came the shame. Partly because he had been called out, and partly because he knew Laila was right.

This was Drew's moment to choose inner work over reactivity. He stepped away, walked the block, practiced deep breathing to regulate his nervous system, wrote down his reactions to better understand them, reconnected with his values, and reminded himself why he does this work. With more clarity, Drew moved into outer work. He didn't rush to fix the optics or issue a vague statement. He got specific. In the following days and months, he made changes that addressed culture, policy, and leadership behavior:

- ◆ He publicly named the harm in a letter to families and conversations with students.
- ◆ He designated and publicized a supervised quiet space for Ramadan observers.
- ◆ He ensured Eid absences would not be penalized and advocated for its inclusion on the calendar.
- ◆ He collaborated with Muslim families and food services to provide halal meal options.

- He updated the dress code to affirm students' rights to wear religious garments.
- He created listening sessions for students and followed up with concrete changes.
- He launched a staff learning series on Islamophobia led by local Muslim educators.

He also revised bullying and harassment protocols to explicitly include religious discrimination. He worked with curriculum teams to integrate lessons that addressed Islamophobia directly and ensured staff were prepared to facilitate them with clarity and care.

He met with the students who caused the harm and their families. He identified the behavior, explained its impact, and, with the support of counselors, led a process of learning and repair. The students reflected on their choices, learned about fasting and Islam, and practiced interrupting their bias.

Finally, Drew turned the lens on adult culture, examining how silence, avoidance, and the absence of clear policies allowed harm to go unchecked. Together, Drew and his staff looked at what needed to change.

Drew's process was honest and accountable. He engaged in inner work to recognize and regulate his emotions, examine his defensiveness, and reconnect with his values. He engaged in outer work using his leadership role to redress harm through structural change. The two are inseparable. Without inner work, his actions may have been reactive. Without outer work, his reflection would have changed nothing.

As equity scholars remind us, equity leadership requires more than noticing harm. It requires redress (Gorski & Swalwell, 2023). It requires us to choose repair over retreat. That choice demands the ability to pause, feel discomfort, and act anyway.

## Reflection Activity: The Inner and Outer Work Reflection Tool

Drew's story illustrates what it means to lead with self-awareness and structural integrity. This tool invites you to begin or deepen your own process.

The tool is anchored in the five SEL domains used throughout the book, integrating inner and outer work for equity-centered leadership.

How to Use This Tool:

- For each statement, ask: *How often is this true for me? What would my team or colleagues say?*
- Notice patterns. Where are you grounded and responsive? Where do you fall into habit, avoid tension, or protect comfort?
- Choose one or two focus areas. Start where it matters most in your context.
- Make a plan. What specific shift will show up in a conversation, meeting, or decision this week?
- Revisit often. Use this tool regularly, not just during crises. Equity leadership is a discipline of reflection, repair, and recommitment.

Use this tool not just to notice, but to disrupt. Leadership is not what we say we value; it's what we repeatedly choose to do.

| **Self-awareness** involves understanding your emotions and how they influence your behavior and relationships. This requires being attuned to physical sensations in your body and being mindful of your thought processes (metacognition). It also encompasses understanding your values, beliefs, and identities, and how they shape your actions and affect how you are perceived in different contexts. ||
|---|---|
| **Inner Work of Self-Awareness** ||
| **Statement** | **Example** |
| I recognize physical sensations in my body and how they connect to my emotions. | Noticing tension in my shoulders while being asked questions about the reasons behind a shift in discipline practices and connecting it to frustration. |
| I identify specific people, characteristics, or experiences that I find challenging or energizing. | Recognizing the difficulty of collaborating with someone resistant to equity work while being energized by a colleague's willingness. |

| | |
|---|---|
| I am aware of my self-limiting beliefs. | Recognizing that a self-limiting belief like "I don't have enough expertise to lead discussions on equity" may be holding me back from facilitating crucial conversations about change within my school community. |
| I notice when I form judgments about people or situations. | Assuming a parent who missed a meeting is uninterested in their child's education. |
| I catch myself when I ruminate on negative thoughts. | Replaying a challenging conversation with a staff member and focusing on what went wrong. |
| I reflect on how my identity influences my thoughts and decisions. | Understanding how my racial identity shapes my views on student behavior. |
| I examine how privilege and power influence my work. | Considering how my role as a principal positions me to challenge inequitable practices. |
| **Outer Work of Social Awareness** | |
| **Statement** | **Example** |
| I seek candid feedback on my actions and decisions. | Asking staff for equity input on a proposed new school policy. |
| I engage in learning about my identities and their impact on others. | Attending an affinity group on antiracism in education. |
| I practice the emotional intelligence skills I want to model. | Showing curiosity instead of defensiveness during critical feedback. |
| I make space for discomfort when learning about inequities. | Participating in community conversations about racial disparities in education. |
| I use my self-awareness to adjust my behavior in the moment. | Recognizing my defensiveness during a meeting and choosing to listen more actively. |
| Self-management is the ability to respond intentionally and purposefully to one's emotions, thoughts, and circumstances to achieve desired behavior, impact, relationships, and/or aspirations. | |
| **Inner Work of Self-Management** | |
| **Statement** | **Example** |
| I create space between my emotions and responses. | Pausing before reacting to a complaint email. |
| I manage my perspective on change. | Viewing policy changes as opportunities for growth. |

| | |
|---|---|
| I adapt my approaches based on feedback. | Reconsidering my facilitation style to allow space for more inclusive participation in meetings. |
| I remain curious about ideas that challenge my beliefs. | Exploring research on alternative grading practices to address inequities. |
| I develop practices to manage stress in high-pressure situations. | Remembering a mantra before starting a challenging discussion. |
| **Outer Work of Self-Management** | |
| I align decisions with my values. | Advocating against a budget cut that would harm students with marginalized identities. |
| I model accountability by following through on commitments. | Completing equity action items agreed upon during a leadership retreat. |
| I challenge inequitable systems or behaviors. | Addressing disproportionate disciplinary actions with staff. |
| I use my positional power to amplify marginalized voices. | Highlighting inequities in a district rezoning proposal meeting and naming the impact on BIPOC students. |
| I navigate challenges with purpose. | Prioritizing resource allocation that supports marginalized students during a budget crisis. |
| **Social awareness** is understanding and empathizing with others, especially those with diverse backgrounds and lived experiences. It calls for a critical grasp of broader historical forces and social norms that shape behaviors across different contexts, challenging us to see not only individuals but the systems that impact them. | |
| **Inner Work of Social Awareness** | |
| **Statement** | **Example** |
| I recognize how my biases influence my perceptions. | Questioning why I perceive some parents as "difficult" and whether my cultural norms play a role. |
| I notice the emotional and power dynamics in groups. | Observing how dominant voices in meetings overshadow quieter ones. |
| I reflect on the impact of my actions on others. | Considering how public praise might unintentionally alienate others or reinforce existing power imbalances. |
| I consider how policies and practices affect marginalized communities. | Evaluating whether school field trip policies unintentionally penalize low-income families. |

| | |
|---|---|
| I consider the relationship between people's behaviors and their experiences and identities. | Reflecting on how a colleague's hesitation to engage in equity work might stem from discomfort with unacknowledged privilege or fear of judgment. |
| I seek to understand how historical and systemic inequities shape current experiences. | Learning about how redlining policies contribute to present-day housing inequities and impact students and families in my school community. |

| Outer Work of Social Awareness | |
|---|---|
| Statement | Example |
| I acknowledge and celebrate the strengths of others. | Amplifying a teacher's equity-focused innovations by integrating them into schoolwide professional development sessions. |
| I use inclusive approaches and materials. | Reviewing curriculum to ensure student identities and perspectives are represented. |
| I support individuals when I notice inequities or harm. | Intervening in microaggressions directed at a student or colleague. |
| I adapt policies to reflect the needs of the communities served. | Revising the parent-teacher conference schedule to accommodate working families. |
| I advocate for systemic changes that promote equity. | Partnering with local organizations to address inequitable access to technology for students. |

**Relationship management** involves establishing and maintaining healthy and supportive relationships with diverse individuals and groups across settings.

This includes listening actively, negotiating conflict constructively, setting boundaries, showing regard for people with differing social and cultural norms, seeking or offering help, and advocating for others when needed.

| Inner Work of Relationship Management | |
|---|---|
| Statement | Example |
| My underlying intention is to have a positive impact on others. | Reflecting on how my approach to equity initiatives acknowledges and validates the lived experiences of marginalized communities. |
| I am willing to cede power to others who can and should share in it. | Considering whose voices must be added to leadership conversations and why. |

| | |
|---|---|
| I am okay with my way not being the best way. | Thinking about how other people's expertise strengthens the organization. |
| I spot and consider how to explore potential conflicts. | Anticipating how power dynamics might influence my listening during conflicts and planning for equitable discussion. |
| I recognize and resist tone policing in myself and others. | Not interrupting or redirecting a staff member who expresses frustration, and recognizing my discomfort with emotion is not a reason to dismiss the message. |
| I consider what conditions would make all stakeholders feel like they have a say in what happens next. | Reflecting on which groups may feel excluded from decision-making and why. |
| **Outer Work of Relationship Management** | |
| **Statement** | **Example** |
| I can build support for important initiatives. | Engaging families, students, and staff in a shared vision for an equity-centered school climate policy through workshops and surveys. |
| I foster open communication and stay receptive to bad and good news. | Encouraging staff to anonymously share concerns about school policies through a feedback form and respond openly during staff meetings. |
| I bring disagreements into the open to support solutions. | Noticing growing frustration among staff about equity policy implementation and initiating a facilitated dialogue to surface concerns and collaboratively address them. |
| I build rapport with wide networks of people regardless of what they have to offer me. | Engaging with non-teaching staff, such as custodians and bus drivers, to learn about their perspectives and build trust. |
| I explore who individuals are outside of the work setting by learning about their interests, passions, goals, and dreams. | Supporting staff social events and ask teachers about their interests and goals. |
| I balance supportive encouragement and critical feedback for all community members (students, colleagues, families). | Acknowledging a team's hard work on an equity initiative while pointing out specific opportunities for improvement in implementation. |

| | |
|---|---|
| I support colleagues and leverage their expertise when challenges arise. | Inviting a teacher with experience in trauma-informed practices to lead a training on supporting students during crises. |
| I celebrate individual and community success, both publicly and privately. | Sending a note to a family thanking them for their involvement in shaping a school equity policy. |
| I protect others from unnecessary emotional labor by taking on relational repair when harm has occurred. | After a student is mocked for their accent, I meet with the student who caused the harm, address it with the whole class, and speak with the teacher about their role. I also check in with the harmed student to affirm their dignity and explain the actions taken. |

Responsible decision-making involves thoughtful, ethical, and constructive personal and social behavior choices. When viewed through an equity lens, it expands beyond individual choices to include an awareness of systemic inequities, a commitment to fairness, and a responsibility to act in ways that disrupt harm and promote justice.

This means that individuals consider the potential consequences of their actions and assess how those decisions affect marginalized and historically excluded groups. It requires reflecting on the power dynamics, questioning whose perspectives are centered or ignored, and ensuring that decisions align with equity-driven values.

**Inner Work of Responsible Decision-Making**

| Statement | Example |
|---|---|
| I analyze whether my decisions reflect my commitment to equity. | Pausing to ask whether a policy decision perpetuates inequities before moving forward. |
| I am intentional about examining my own biases before making a decision. | Reflecting on how my implicit assumptions might shape hiring recommendations. |
| I acknowledge when my past decisions have caused harm and commit to repair. | Addressing inequitable discipline policies by openly revising them and seeking community input. |
| I sit with discomfort and complexity when navigating challenging decisions. | Taking time to fully understand multiple perspectives in a heated discussion rather than rushing to a decision. |
| I evaluate how my decisions align with the voices and needs of marginalized communities. | Seeking feedback from underrepresented groups before finalizing an initiative. |
| I am committed to continuous self-reflection and learning to improve my decision-making. | Regularly engaging with professional development on equity-centered leadership. |

| | |
|---|---|
| I recognize when I'm prioritizing comfort over equity or systemic change. | Resisting the urge to avoid conflict by choosing easier but inequitable paths. |
| I critically evaluate whether proposed solutions address root causes of inequities. | Questioning whether a new diversity training initiative is masking deeper organizational issues. |
| I resist token gestures and focus on systemic, impactful actions. | Prioritizing long-term equity policies over performative public statements. |
| I seek to understand and question the dominant norms and structures influencing my decisions. | Identifying how a policy might privilege dominant cultural values. |
| **Outer Work of Responsible Decision-Making** | |
| I center decisions on the needs and voices of those most impacted by inequity. | Inviting community members to co-create solutions rather than imposing top-down changes. |
| I use data and evidence to identify inequities and inform decisions. | Analyzing student performance trends to uncover disparities before implementing academic interventions. |
| I challenge policies, practices, or traditions that perpetuate inequities. | Advocating to eliminate tracking systems that disproportionately harm marginalized students. |
| I ensure decisions promote accountability and transparency. | Publicly sharing the rationale and expected outcomes for major decisions. |
| I actively involve stakeholders with diverse perspectives in decision-making processes. | Establishing advisory committees that include students, families, and staff from different backgrounds. |
| I set measurable goals for equity-focused outcomes and track progress. | Defining specific metrics to evaluate the impact of a discipline reform policy. |
| I avoid detours that focus on optics over substance. | Steering conversations away from superficial celebrations to address systemic barriers. |
| I model ethical and courageous decision-making for others. | Speaking up in meetings to advocate for equitable practices, even when it's unpopular or professionally risky. |
| I assess how decisions impact the broader community, not just immediate stakeholders. | Considering how changes to hiring practices might influence representation in the long term. |
| I create and sustain structures that foster collaborative and equitable decision-making. | Implementing team norms that prioritize shared decision-making and equity audits. |

# Conclusion
# Belonging Without Exception

This book is about the inner and outer work of equity-centered leadership, about making decisions that align with our values, even when they're hard, even when they come at a cost. This moment in education demands such leadership. But truly, when hasn't it?

Throughout the writing of this book, Palestinian and Arab children who attend our schools are watching people like them, sometimes their family members, being killed in real time, through livestreamed videos and media coverage. In the wake of the October 7, 2023 Hamas attack in Israel and the ensuing Israeli response of genocide in Gaza, the Council on American-Islamic Relations (CAIR) reported a 180% increase in complaints regarding Islamophobia, anti-Arab discrimination, and anti-Palestinian racism, many from students and families in school communities. The unspoken but deeply felt message to educators has been clear. Don't talk about it. Don't talk about them. Don't create space for learning, discussion, or emotional processing. I've felt that message firsthand.

Just as educators have been discouraged from naming racism, white supremacy, or settler colonialism, we're now told—implicitly or explicitly—not to acknowledge Palestinian suffering or criticize Israeli policy and practice. In some schools, doing so is quickly labeled antisemitic, blurring the line between hate speech and equity-centered discourse. The effect is the same: honest conversation shuts down. Our students carry the cost of that silence, particularly those already rendered invisible by dominant narratives.

I've written this book with the hope that every student's identity, history, and experience will belong in our schools. We cannot claim to lead equity-centered organizations while erasing or excluding some voices to protect the comfort of others, or ourselves. Just as we cannot teach this country's history while excluding Black and Indigenous histories and voices, we cannot ignore or erase Arab, Muslim, or Palestinian histories, cultures, beliefs, or emotions from our classrooms.

When we do, we send a message about who belongs and who doesn't. We normalize exclusion and create conditions where some students are safe, seen, and supported, while others are treated as invisible, threatening, or less than human. Such selective inclusion undermines every equity commitment we claim to hold.

Many educators are under pressure right now from their communities, their school boards, and their fear of saying the wrong thing. I don't have an easy answer for that. But I do know this: silence is not neutral.

I wrestled with the decision to write this conclusion. I worried that naming the harm facing Palestinian, Arab, and Muslim students, or even using the word "genocide," the language used by UN experts, genocide scholars, and the International Court of Justice, could cost me professionally. I considered that some people might think I'm antisemitic. I even debated mentioning that my husband is Jewish, as if that might give me credibility or cover. I spent a disproportionate number of hours on just a few sentences in the book's introduction, trying to get the wording about the othering of Palestinians and Muslims "right."

How could I write a book asking school and district leaders to lead with courage and clarity, then sidestep that responsibility myself? This work begins with the inner work of noticing when fear, silence, or self-protective stories creep in, and continues with the outer work of choosing to act in alignment with our values, whether it is risky or not. Like most of us, I wrestle with speaking up when it's inconvenient, unpopular, or uncomfortable. I, too, struggle to confront the places where I soften the message or tell myself the timing isn't right.

Each chapter in this book offered reflection and a commitment, something to hold ourselves accountable to. Together, these chapter-based commitments form the backbone of equity-centered leadership:

- ◆ Introduction:
  I commit to integrating inner reflection with outward action, recognizing that equity requires both personal transformation and systemic change.
- ◆ Chapter 1 – A Tiered Approach Starts with All Students in Mind:
  I commit to centering student voice, identity, and agency in Tier 1 practices, ensuring SEL reflects all students' cultural realities, not dominant norms.
- ◆ Chapter 2 – Creating the Conditions for SEL:
  I commit to designing environments where all students experience belonging, autonomy, and competence.
- ◆ Chapter 3 – Self-Awareness:
  I commit to examining how my emotions, biases, identity, and leadership behaviors shape the school community, and to aligning my intentions with my actual impact.
- ◆ Chapter 4 – Self-Management:
  I commit to using cognitive, somatic, and self-care strategies to manage my reactions and regulate emotions to respond to inequity with clarity and courage.
- ◆ Chapter 5 – Social Awareness:
  I commit to recognizing how identity and power shape interactions and making context-responsive decisions that balance technical solutions with relational insight.
- ◆ Chapter 6 – Relationship Management:
  I commit to navigating trust, conflict, and power dynamics in ways that sustain principled leadership and support change across systems, not just individuals.

- ◆ Chapter 7 – Responsible Decision-Making:
  I commit to making values-driven decisions that protect students with marginalized identities and redress inequity, even when those choices are unpopular, risky, or professionally costly.
- ◆ Chapter 8 – Putting It Into Practice:
  I commit to returning to self-reflection as a leadership discipline. I will use what I learn to disrupt inequitable patterns and act in ways that advance justice.

These commitments are not a checklist. They're a practice, one that asks us to return, again and again, to our purpose and our courage.

This book is for leaders ready to move beyond performative equity statements and into the real, messy, and deeply human work of leading with social and emotional intelligence, clarity, and purpose. If it has done anything, I hope it has reminded us that our voices matter. Our choices matter—even the small ones. And in moments like these, our silence or our willingness to speak not only shapes the conditions of our schools but also exposes the values we model for the young people watching us.

# Bibliography

Aguilar, Elena. *Coaching for Equity: Conversations That Change Practice.* 1st ed., Jossey-Bass, 2020.

Aguilar, Elena. *The Art of Coaching Teams: Building Resilient Communities That Transform Schools.* Jossey-Bass, 2016.

Barrett, Lisa Feldman. *How Emotions Are Made: The Secret Life of the Brain.* Mariner Books, 2017.

Barrett, Lisa Feldman. *Seven and a Half Lessons About the Brain.* Houghton Mifflin Harcourt, 2021.

Boyatzis, Richard E. "Intentional Change Theory: Explanation and Implications for the Management of Change." *Organization Development: A Jossey-Bass Reader*, edited by Joan V. Gallos, Jossey-Bass, 2006, pp. 607–618.

Brown, Penelope. *Adaptive Leadership: A Perspective on Transforming Education.* Centre for Strategic Education, Leading Education Series No. 15, Apr. 2023.

Center for Black Educator Development. *State of the Black Educator Pipeline Report.* Center for Black Educator Development, 2023.

Cohn-Vargas, Becki, Kelli Kahn, and Amy Epstein. Identity Safe Classrooms, Grades 6–12: *Pathways to Belonging and Learning for Teens.* Corwin, 2020.

Collaborative for Academic, Social, and Emotional Learning. *CASEL's SEL Framework: What Are the Core Competence Areas and Where Are*

*They Promoted?* CASEL, 1 Oct. 2020, casel.org/casel-sel-framework-11-2020/.

Copur-Gencturk, Yasemin, In-Hee Thacker, and Andrei Cimpian. "How Teachers' Beliefs About Gender Equality Relate to Their Math Instruction and Student Participation." *Educational Researcher*, vol. 52, no. 1, 2023, pp. 48–60. https://doi.org/10.3102/0013189X221129692.

Crenshaw, Kimberlé. "Demarginalizing the Intersection of Race and Sex: A Black Feminist Critique of Antidiscrimination Doctrine, Feminist Theory and Antiracist Politics." *University of Chicago Legal Forum*, vol. 1989, no. 1, 1989, pp. 139–167.

Darling-Hammond, Linda, et al. "Implications for Educational Practice of the Science of Learning and Development." *Applied Developmental Science*, vol. 24, no. 2, 2020, pp. 97–140. https://doi.org/10.1080/10888691.2018.1537791.

Darling-Hammond, Sean, and Eric Ho. "No Matter How You Slice It, Black Students Are Punished More: The Persistence and Pervasiveness of Discipline Disparities." *AERA Open*, vol. 10, 2024, p. 23328584241293411.

de Boer, Hester, Thea H. van der Werf, and Roel J. Bosker. "The Effects of Teacher Expectancy on Student Achievement: A Meta-analysis." *Educational Research Review*, vol. 35, 2022, 100433. https://doi.org/10.1016/j.edurev.2022.100433.

De Boer, Hester, et al. "The Effect of Teacher Expectations on Student Outcomes: A Meta-Analysis." *Educational Research Review*, vol. 37, 2022, p. 100461. https://doi.org/10.1016/j.edurev.2022.100461.

Deci, Edward L., and Richard M. Ryan. *Self-Determination Theory: Basic Psychological Needs in Motivation, Development, and Wellness*. Guilford Press, 2020.

DiAngelo, Robin. *White Fragility: Why It's So Hard for White People to Talk About Racism*. Beacon Press, 2018.

Edmondson, Amy C. *Right Kind of Wrong: The Science of Failing Well*. Atria Books, 2023.

Eurich, Tasha. *Insight: The Surprising Truth About How Others See Us, How We See Ourselves, and Why the Answers Matter More Than We Think*. Crown Business, 2018.

Flavell, John H. "Metacognition and Cognitive Monitoring: A New Area of Cognitive–Developmental Inquiry." *American Psychologist*, vol. 34, no. 10, 1979, pp. 906–911. https://doi.org/10.1037/0003-066X.34.10.906.

Ford, Brett Q., and Allison S. Troy. "Reappraisal Reconsidered: A Closer Look at the Costs of an Acclaimed Emotion-Regulation Strategy." *Current Directions in Psychological Science*, vol. 28, no. 2, 2019, pp. 195–203. https://doi.org/10.1177/0963721419827315.

Geronimus, Arline T. *Weathering: The Extraordinary Stress of Ordinary Life in an Unjust Society*. Little, Brown Spark, 2023.

Ginwright, Shawn. *The Four Pivots: Reimagining Justice, Reimagining Ourselves*. North Atlantic Books, 2022.

GLSEN. *Erasure and Resilience: The Experiences of LGBTQ Students of Color*. GLSEN, 2021.

Gobodo-Madikizela, Pumla. *Aesthetics of Memory: Repair, Reconciliation, and the Arts*. Yale University Press, 2024.

Goleman, Daniel, Richard Boyatzis, and Annie McKee. *Primal Leadership: Unleashing the Power of Emotional Intelligence*. Harvard Business Review Press, 2013.

Goodenow, Carol, and Kathleen E. Grady. "The Relationship of School Belonging and Friends' Values to Academic Motivation Among Urban Adolescent Students." *The Journal of Experimental Education*, vol. 62, no. 1, 1993, pp. 60–71.

Gorski, Paul C. "How Trauma-Informed Are We, Really?" *Equity Literacy Institute*, 2020. www.equityliteracy.org/trauma-informed.

Gorski, Paul C. *Reaching and Teaching Students in Poverty: Strategies for Erasing the Opportunity Gap*. Teachers College Press, 2019.

Gorski, Paul C., and Katy Swalwell. "Equity Literacy as an Antidote to Inequity in Schools." *Educational Leadership*, vol. 78, no. 6, 2021, pp. 64–69.

Gorski, Paul C., and Katy Swalwell. *Equity Literacy for All: Dismantling Inequities in Schools and Beyond*. Harvard Education Press, 2024.

Gorski, Paul C., and Katy Swalwell. *Fix Injustice, Not Kids and Other Principles for Transformative Equity Leadership*. ASCD, 2023.

Gross, James J., and Oliver P. John. "Individual Differences in Two Emotion Regulation Processes: Implications for Affect, Relationships, and Well-Being." *Journal of Personality and Social Psychology*, vol. 85, no. 2, 2003, pp. 348–362. https://doi.org/10.1037/0022-3514.85.2.348.

Gullo, Anthony D., and Floyd D. Beachum. "Unconscious Bias in Schools: A Developmental Approach to Exploring Race and Racism." *International Journal of Educational Leadership Preparation*, vol. 15, no. 1, 2020, pp. 30–47.

Harris, Angelique. *Burnout in the Margins: Strategies for Sustaining Work Toward Justice*. Beacon Press, 2023.

Harris, Farah. *The Color of Emotional Intelligence: Elevating Our Self and Social Awareness to Address Inequities*. Wiley, 2023.

Heifetz, Ronald A., and Marty Linsky. *Leadership on the Line: Staying Alive Through the Dangers of Change*. Revised ed., Harvard Business Review Press, 2017.

hooks, bell. *Belonging: A Culture of Place*. Routledge, 2009.

Huizar, Diana, Zoey Phillips, and Paul Gorski. "Adult SEL and the Racial Equity Imperative: Three Key Commitments." *Intercultural Education*, vol. 36, no. 2, 2025, pp. 146–161.

Jagers, Robert J., Deborah Rivas-Drake, and Teresa Borowski. "Transformative Social and Emotional Learning (SEL): Toward SEL in Service of Educational Equity and Excellence." *American Educational Research Association*, 2018.

Jagers, Robert J., Deborah Rivas-Drake, and Brittney Williams. "Transformative Social and Emotional Learning (SEL): Toward SEL in Service of Educational Equity and Excellence." *Educational Psychologist*, vol. 54, no. 3, 2019, pp. 162–184. Taylor & Francis Online, https://doi.org/10.1080/00461520.2019.1623032.

Jones, Stephanie M., and Suzanne M. Bouffard. "Social and Emotional Learning in Schools: From Programs to Strategies and Commentaries." *Journal of School Health*, vol. 82, no. 12, 2012, pp. 576–585. https://doi.org/10.1002/j.2379-3988.2012.tb00073.x.: contentReference{index=133}.

Jones, Stephanie M., et al. *Navigating Social and Emotional Learning from the Inside Out: Looking Inside & Across 33 Leading SEL Programs: A Practical Resource for Schools and OST Providers (Preschool & Elementary Focus)*. 2nd ed., Wallace Foundation, 2021.

Katie, Byron, and Stephen Mitchell. *Loving What Is: Four Questions That Can Change Your Life*. Harmony Books, 2002.

Kendi, Ibram X. *How to Be an Antiracist*. One World, 2019.

Kidder, Rushworth M. *Moral Courage*. William Morrow, 2005.

Liu, Dongdong, et al. "Emotion Contagion in Organizations: A Meta-Analytic Review of Affective Linkages in Teams and Leader–Follower Dyads." *Journal of Applied Psychology*, vol. 107, no. 7, 2022, pp. 1168–1196. https://doi.org/10.1037/apl0000907.

Livingston, Robert. *The Conversation: How Seeking and Speaking the Truth About Racism Can Radically Transform Individuals and Organizations*. Currency, 2020.

Losen, Daniel J., and Harold Jordan. *Disabling Inequity: The Urgent Need for Race-Conscious Education Policy*. The Center for Civil Rights Remedies, UCLA, 2021. https://civilrightsproject.ucla.edu/research/k-12-education/school-discipline/discipline-disparities-research-to-practice/disabling-inequity-the-urgent-need-for-race-conscious-education-policy.

Madda, Mary Jo. "Dena Simmons: Without Context, Social-Emotional Learning Can Backfire." *EdSurge*, 15 May 2019, edsurge.com/news/2019-05-15-dena-simmons-without-context-social-emotional-learning-can-backfire.

Menakem, Resmaa. *My Grandmother's Hands: Racialized Trauma and the Pathway to Mending Our Hearts and Bodies*. Central Recovery Press, 2017.

Morris, Monique W. *Sing a Rhythm, Dance a Blues: Education for the Liberation of Black and Brown Girls*. The New Press, 2019.

Nevarez, Michele. *Beyond Emotional Intelligence: A Guide to Accessing Your Full Potential*. Wiley, 2022.

Owens, Ann. "Racial Disparities in School Discipline: The Role of Teacher Narratives." *Sociology of Education*, vol. 96, no. 2, 2023, pp. 123–39. https://doi.org/10.1177/00380407231153216.

Panorama Education. "What Is MTSS?" Panorama Education. www.panoramaed.com/blog/mtss-comprehensive-guide.

Peifer, Corinna, et al. "A Scoping Review of Flow Research." *Frontiers in Psychology*, vol. 13, 2022, Article 815665. https://doi.org/10.3389/fpsyg.2022.815665.

Rivas-Drake, Deborah, et al. "Examining the Role of Racial Identity and Racialized Experiences in the Development of Adolescents' Intergroup Attitudes." *Child Development Perspectives*, vol. 17, no. 1, 2023, pp. 32–38. https://doi.org/10.1111/cdep.12494.

Rosenthal, Robert, and Lenore Jacobson. *Pygmalion in the Classroom: Teacher Expectation and Pupils' Intellectual Development*. Holt, Rinehart and Winston, 1968.

Ryan, Michelle K., S. Alexander Haslam, and Floor Rink. "Why Women Are More Likely Than Men to Pursue Risky Leadership Roles." *Harvard Business Review*, Jan.–Feb. 2022.

Ryan, Richard M., and Edward L. Deci. "Intrinsic and Extrinsic Motivation from a Self-Determination Theory Perspective: Definitions, Theory, Practices, and Future Directions." *Contemporary Educational Psychology*, vol. 61, Apr. 2020, p. 101860. https://doi.org/10.1016/j.cedpsych.2020.101860.

Scott, Kim. *Radical Candor: Be a Kick-Ass Boss Without Losing Your Humanity*. St. Martin's Press, 2017.

Sensoy, Özlem, and Robin DiAngelo. *Is Everyone Really Equal?: An Introduction to Key Concepts in Social Justice Education*. 2nd ed., Teachers College Press, 2017.

Simmons, Dena. "5 Questions with Dena Simmons." *Loyola University Chicago*, 2021. www.luc.edu/features/stories/academics/denasimmons/.

Simmons, Dena. "Why SEL Alone Isn't Enough." *Educational Leadership*, vol. 78, no. 6, Mar. 2021, pp. 30–34.

Steele, Claude M. *Stereotype Threat: Intellectual Test Performance and the Social Identity Threat*. Harvard University Press, 2021.

Tanase, Madalina, and Paul Gorski. "Personal Deficiency, Racism, or Culture Clash?: Teacher Candidates' Beliefs About Why Racial Discipline Disparities Exist." *Teaching and Teacher Education*, vol. 110, 2022, p. 103596. https://doi.org/10.1016/j.tate.2021.103596.

Tatum, Beverly Daniel. "The Complexity of Identity: 'Who Am I?'" 2018.

Tatum, Beverly Daniel. *Why Are All the Black Kids Sitting Together in the Cafeteria?: And Other Conversations About Race*. 5th anniversary ed., Basic Books, 2017.

Taylor, Dorceta E. *Toxic Communities: Environmental Racism, Industrial Pollution, and Residential Mobility*. NYU Press, 2020.

Taylor, Matthew. *The Noble School Leader: The Five-Square Approach to Leading Schools with Emotional Intelligence*. Corwin, 2022.

Troy, Allison S., and Brett Q. Ford. "Change What You Can: Emotion Regulation Is More Effective for Emotions Linked to Malleable Outcomes." *Psychological Science*, vol. 31, no. 7, 2020, pp. 944–56. https://doi.org/10.1177/0956797620916784.

U.S. Government Accountability Office. *K–12 Education: Student Experiences with Bullying, Hate Speech, Hate Crimes, and Related Discipline*. GAO-22-104341, 2022.

van de Weijer-Bergsma, Eva, et al. *Effects of Mindfulness-Based Practices on Children's Self-Regulation: A Review on Early Childhood Research*, 2024. www.researchgate.net/publication/377853126.

Walton, Gregory M., and Geoffrey L. Cohen. "A Brief Social-Belonging Intervention Improves Academic and Health Outcomes of Minority Students." *Science*, vol. 331, no. 6023, 2011, pp. 1447–51.

Xie, Xiaofei, Xiang He, and Yiqun Gan. "Leader–Member Emotion Contagion and Follower Outcomes: A Meta-Analytic Review." *Journal of Organizational Behavior*, vol. 42, no. 7, 2021, pp. 1005–21. https://doi.org/10.1002/job.2524.

Zheng, Lily. *DEI Deconstructed: Your No-Bullsht Guide to Diversity, Equity, and Inclusion*. Berrett-Koehler Publishers, 2021.

For Product Safety Concerns and Information please contact our EU
representative  GPSR@taylorandfrancis.com
Taylor & Francis Verlag GmbH, Kaufingerstraße 24, 80331 München, Germany

www.ingramcontent.com/pod-product-compliance
Lightning Source LLC
Chambersburg PA
CBHW070805230426
43665CB00017B/2499